People's Friend

Contents

Complete Stories

P164

P36

P147

P13

Annual 1999

The Farmer And His Wife by John Taylor

P10

J. Campbell Kerr Paintings

Verse 'n' Views

Dear Reader,

I'm delighted to welcome you to "The People's Friend Annual 1999." Happy new 1999 from all of us at the "Friend"!

In this year's Annual you'll find a whole host of entertaining reading, with over 20 new complete Stories sure to delight, amuse or touch your heart. All are by popular "Friend" writers.

"Friend" favourite Colin Gibson has compiled an almanac of tales to take you through the whole of the new year. There are also great views to enjoy from the palette of cover artist J. Campbell Kerr. And, as you turn the pages, you'll discover a wealth of poetic gems, to suit every mood.

So, settle down and relax with your special "Friend."

The Editor

The Winning Bet

by Mariana Woolley

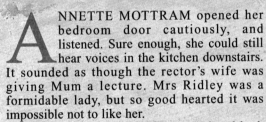

ANNETTE MOTTRAM opened her bedroom door cautiously, and listened. Sure enough, she could still hear voices in the kitchen downstairs. It sounded as though the rector's wife was giving Mum a lecture. Mrs Ridley was a formidable lady, but so good hearted it was impossible not to like her.

The kitchen door suddenly opened and both ladies came out into the hall.

"But, Gwen," Emily Ridley had a voice as commanding as her presence, "she's not even looking for another job."

"It's only a fortnight, you know." Her mother sounded apologetic. "She's taking a holiday first."

Annette shut her bedroom door quietly and slumped into the chair by the open window.

Why couldn't they leave her alone? She quickly revised her opinion of Emily Ridley — she was a bossy busybody!

She gazed out at the blue sky. It was a heavenly day. But she was in no mood to enjoy it.

"After all —" Mrs Ridley had obviously paused under the bedroom window "— she's not the only girl to have been made redundant. I know it's bad luck that young man chose to finish with her shortly afterwards. But, I don't mind telling you, I don't believe that was a coincidence. If you ask me, she's well rid of him!"

Annette slammed the window shut and flung herself furiously on to the bed, angry tears filling her eyes. How could they? Ron had written her such a beautiful, heart-breaking letter. She's shown it to no-one, not even Mum.

My dear girl,

You must forget me. I can't hold you to a promise made when we were both independent and full of hope for the future.

You have enough worries without having to bear the burden of a miserable out-of-work misfit. So it's goodbye, my own darling. Don't try to get in touch — I couldn't bear it.

I'm leaving the district and, at the moment, don't even know where I'm going or what I'll do . . .

Your always faithful, Ron.

How could they say such awful things about him? He'd been so sympathetic when she'd told him about her job; advised her what to do with her redundancy money. He'd even taken her out for supper to cheer her up.

Then Annette suddenly remembered, uncomfortably, that he still owed her for the rather expensive meal. She shut her mind to that firmly, dried her eyes, freshened her make-up, and ran downstairs, intending to have it out with her mother.

Gwen Mottram disarmed her at once by apologising both for herself and her friend.

"It's because I love you," she said coaxingly. "And Emily is fond of you, too, she really is.

"I just can't help worrying. Not about the money side," she added hastily. "I just hate to see you moping and unhappy."

Annette's conscience pricked her.

"OK," she said, grudgingly. "I'll look for a job after the weekend. I just felt I deserved a little break first."

"I don't suppose you could help Emily Ridley with some of her visiting?" Gwen asked tentatively. "Her nephew, Sandy McKay — you remember Sandy? — is coming for a fortnight's holiday. She wants to have some spare time for him."

Annette's heart sank.

"Of course I remember Sandy. Horrid little boy!" She looked sideways at her mother and, in spite of herself, grinned.

"So that's what you were hatching up together, was it? I might have known. I suppose I'll have to say yes to that tiresome woman. Who does she want me to visit?"

"Ada Saunders for one," Gwen confessed, "and —"

"Ada Saunders!" Annette knew her by her reputation.

"I know she's not the most — er, friendly person, but she does need visiting at the moment. She broke a hip about three weeks ago and is still on crutches. You don't mend so quickly when you're over seventy, you know. She needs someone to fetch her shopping, help with the housework — that sort of thing."

"I think," Annette said, "I'd better talk to Mrs Ridley myself. I'll help out where I can, but I draw the line at Ada Saunders! She can make her wonderful Sandy do it for her," she added vindictively.

ANNETTE remembered Sandy from school, though he, at three or four years older, had been in a higher class. He really had been a horrid boy. She wasn't the only one he'd reduced to tears of rage!

Thank goodness they'd hardly seen each other since she'd completed her secretarial course and he'd decided to go to police college.

When they did meet, he was just the same — teasing, provoking and too good looking to be true. He thought her spoilt, she knew.

"If I am spoilt," she'd once said to him furiously, "I didn't spoil myself!"

"And I'm not going to either," he'd retorted.

"When's Sandy coming?" she wondered aloud.

"Tomorrow. Why don't you go to see Emily now? I know she's home this afternoon."

Annette glanced at her watch.

"I won't go now — all the Mums will be waiting outside the school."

"What's wrong with that?" Her mother was puzzled.

"They'll ask me how I am, what I'm going to do. Is it true? Etc. No, thanks!"

"You've got to face it some time. The longer you leave it, the worse it'll be."

"The longer I leave it, the more they'll forget. I'll go the the rectory early tomorrow morning, before Sandy arrives."

Gwen sighed, shrugged, and said no more.

Annette heard the sigh and glanced up quickly. She suddenly realised that her mother looked tired.

"What time will Dad be back tonight, Mum?"

"About seven, he said."

"Like me to do the supper?"

Gwen hesitated, looking speculatively at her daughter, and then accepted gratefully.

"I thought we'd just have mince . . ."

For the first time in two weeks Annette's spirits rose. She enjoyed cooking and, though she wouldn't acknowledge it, she was beginning to feel rather fed up. She'd obviously been relying too heavily on her mother and she vowed to make more of an effort to help out around the house.

True to her word, Annette set off for the rectory at about 8.15 the next

The Rabbit

by John Taylor

I PULLED back our bedroom curtains the other morning and was surprised to see a rabbit nibbling at some of Anne's plants.

"Anne, there's a friend of yours in the garden."

"John, you said you had got rid of that mole."

I didn't let on it was a rabbit.

Anne swung out of bed and came to the window.

"Humph — a rabbit," she said, and then gave it a loud, "Shoo!"

It looked up and then disappeared.

I think I told you that we had

trouble with a mole. I looked out one morning and discovered a mole had made one of its earth heaps in our garden. Well, before I got round to dealing with it, one heap had become four!

I was told in no uncertain terms that I would have to do something about our visiting rabbit.

Of course, that was easier said than done. I haven't a gun any longer and, to be honest, I wasn't a very good shot at the best of times.

I'd actually been surprised to see that rabbit on the lawn, as I haven't seen one on the farm for a few weeks.

I was, as a youngster, an expert at setting snares. Early in the morning, I'd check my snares. Any rabbits caught were strung on my handlebars and sold to our local butcher. The price given was between sixpence and a shilling, and it

day. But when she cycled into the drive, she felt a spasm of irritation. There was a brand-new motorbike parked outside the front door.

Annette went round to the back and, sure enough, there was Sandy eating a hearty breakfast with his uncle and aunt. She would have retreated at once, but the rector saw her and beckoned her in.

"Coffee?" he offered cheerfully. "Tea? Here's Sandy. You remember Sandy?"

"Of course I remember Sandy!" She pinned a smile on her face.

Sandy got up.

"Well, if it isn't our Annie!"

So, he'd remembered from school days how she hated her name to be shortened.

went into the Savings Bank. In those days, a shilling was money not to be squandered.

Anne also sold rabbits. She went with her father, in their trap, to Cupar on a Tuesday, with a basket filled with butter she'd made, eggs, and fowls that had been plucked — and any rabbits caught by her father or brothers.

I always think there's nothing nicer than a rabbit pie, with thick gravy and a pastry top.

For some reason, Anne didn't go into town one market day, but gave me a shopping list. I had to visit the butcher's and, on the spur of the moment, I asked if he had a rabbit for sale.

"Sorry, John, no fresh ones today, only frozen."

Why bother to freeze the humble rabbit? I thought he was pulling my leg. He wasn't. His rabbits had been imported from China!

I didn't buy a Chinese rabbit. Somehow, I don't think it would have tasted the same.

I F I read something in a paper or magazine that interests me about Fife, I cut it out and put it away in a box file. I have by now a number of such files.

I knew I had some cuttings about rabbits in Fife, so fetched down the most likely file. I didn't find the one I was looking for, but spent an enjoyable evening reading my cuttings.

Anne must have been thinking about my search for that cutting about rabbits.

At breakfast next day she said she had remembered seeing a report from the Forestry Commission about land near Tentsmuir in Fife. I knew where that would be filed and found it.

The Forestry Commission were wanting to expand their forest and the paper I had acquired, I don't know how, was an acquisition report on the land in years gone by.

In the report it states:

Assessed rental £370 per annum, which includes rabbit trapping.

The grazing is of very little value, having been destroyed by the great number of rabbits. These have been a very valuable asset, the proceeds from which last year (1924) came to about £600.

It also states that the previous year the proprietor of this area sold rabbits to the value of £900!

Coming back to that rabbit in Anne's garden, I had better track it down. Rabbits can breed all the year round and if it finds a mate there is no knowing how many we might have on the Riggin by this time next year!

The Farmer And His Wife

She flushed slightly and held out a hand.

"How are you, Alexander?" He disliked his full name.

"Touché," he murmured and grinned disarmingly.

Annette turned to Emily Ridley.

"Mum said you wanted me to do some visiting for you. I will, though I have to admit —" she laughed self-consciously "— I don't get on with all the old folk in the village."

Sandy leaned back in his chair.

"For instance, you daren't tackle our redoubtable Ada Saunders?" he mocked. "Can't blame you. She's too much for most folk."

Annette rose to the bait.

"As for poor old Mrs Saunders, I'm not in the least afraid of her. Of course, if she needs help, I'm more than willing to offer."

"I bet though, that she's one of the old folk you don't get on with."

She swallowed the bait — hook, line and sinker.

"Look here, Sandy McKay —" she burst out furiously "— I bet you, before your holiday is over, Ada Saunders and I will be the best of friends!"

"Taken!" Sandy laughed triumphantly. "I bet you dinner at the Golden Pheasant that you won't be on speaking terms with her before the end of the fortnight."

"Done!"

THE beautiful weather held and Annette set off bright and early next morning to begin her visits. I'll do Ada Saunders first, she thought. Get it over and done with.

She approached the cottage slowly and knocked tentatively on the front door. No answer.

Probably, as was usual in the village, the front door was less used than the back. She followed the path round to the kitchen entrance, and peeped in through the window.

Sure enough, Ada was sitting in a chair by the stove, wrapped in an old dressing-gown, her crutches beside her. She looked very forbidding as she glanced crossly at Annette, and beckoned her in.

"You're early," she greeted her uncompromisingly.

"I'm sorry. Am I too early?"

"Yes, you are. I'm not dressed yet. I haven't had my breakfast."

"Can I help you dress?"

"No, you can't. If Nurse can't manage it, it's not likely a slip of a girl could. Who are you, anyway?"

Annette felt herself flush.

"I'm Mrs Mottram's daughter," she replied stiffly.

"Oh. The one who's just had the sack, eh? So that's why you're doing Nurse's job for her."

Annette bridled.

"Nurse is busy with this flu epidemic and three new babies in the village," she protested.

"As if I would take up much of anyone's time," the old lady said tartly. "You can go now, and come back in about an hour," she ordered.

Annette was bubbling with suppressed exasperation, but at the same time felt pleased with herself. She'd faced the worst and kept her temper.

But if it wasn't for Sandy, I'd never go near her again, she thought fiercely.

After about an hour and a half, she went back to the cottage and found Mrs Saunders waiting for her, dressed, and drinking a cup of tea.

She nodded ungraciously.

"I don't need anything this morning. If you come tomorrow, I'd like my order fetched from the store. You could call in at the shop on your way here, come to that. It's on your road."

"Yes, I could do that."

"They know my order. I'll give you the money when you bring it. I'm assuming you *are* coming tomorrow. Or are you like all the rest — one good deed a month?" She laughed disagreeably.

Annette went to the door.

"Yes, I'll be coming tomorrow," she said shortly, and went out.

Sandy McKay was waiting for her at the gate.

"Well, still alive? You weren't long in there, were you? Chased you out, did she?"

"She didn't need me this morning."

His mocking smile got her back up.

"Look here, Sandy McKay, I've promised your aunt I'll help out with the visiting, and so I will. Why don't you leave me alone, and find someone else to annoy? If you must know, I can't stand you — and never could!"

Her words sounded childish, even to her own ears. She mounted her bicycle and peddled off furiously, his laughter ringing in her ears.

Yet her attack had the desired effect. There was no sign of Sandy when she went to the store for Mrs Saunders' order the next day.

One or two people asked how she was. She was surprised by how easy it was to talk to them — everyone was very sympathetic.

"Any luck with a job yet?"

"I've got an eye open. But I'm keeping busy — I'm helping Mrs Ridley with visiting at the moment."

"How are you getting on with old Mrs Saunders?" There was general good-natured laughter in the shop, and Annette gave a rueful smile as the local district nurse spoke.

"She's a cough drop, and no mistake. But I reckon the poor old thing is lonely and unhappy." Trust Nurse to throw in a kind word! "Take no notice of the bark! She won't really bite!"

Annette gathered up the order and, when she arrived at the back door, Mrs Saunders was waiting for her.

"Put it on the table . . . Thank you. I'll check the things with my list. They're not always reliable at the shop."

"Oh, don't you think so? We've always found them entirely dependable."

"You're lucky. Or easy going," Mrs Saunders snapped sourly.

Annette said nothing.

"Here's the money. Everything seems all right, for once.

"Nurse comes tomorrow to bath me, so you needn't bother."

No Mrs S. tomorrow! It'd be like a holiday!

Now what shall I do tomorrow, Annette thought luxuriously. I could give Mum a hand in the house. Or the garden . . . or both even! She would have been surprised if she'd realised that Ron hadn't been in her thoughts for nearly three days.

Annette was up in time to have breakfast with her father, the first time for more than two weeks, and offered cheerfully to go to the shop for the groceries. On the way back, she met Nurse.

"I've just been to old Mrs Saunders. My word, you've made a hit there!"

Annette's jaw dropped and she stared incredulously at Nurse.

"You've got to be joking!"

"No, it's the truth. She says you're reliable. The highest praise! You ought to be a social worker, my dear. You're wasted in an office." She laughed comfortably and drove off.

There must be some mistake, Annette thought. But, all the same, it was with a new spirit of confidence that she went back home with the groceries.

Sandy poked his head above the rectory hedge, which he was tackling with a pair of shears.

"Off the hook today?"

Annette nodded quite amiably.

"I don't mind telling you," she confided, "it's heavenly to have a day off."

"Nose to the grindstone tomorrow?"

"Of course." She grinned. "I'm looking forward to my free dinner."

"There's still a week to go," he warned her, and went back to trimming the hedge.

ADA SAUNDERS seemed more relaxed on her next visit. Annette had brought her a bag of ripe plums and, for a moment, the old eyes brightened with pleasure.

The kitten was a help, too. It had strayed from next door and bounced into the kitchen, treating the old lady as a privileged friend. It clawed its way up her leg and played engagingly with the fringe of her shawl.

"Shall I take it back?"

"No. Leave it for a moment. It's nice to have a bit of young life about."

So the kitten stayed for a good half hour. So did Annette, her spirits rising higher, her confidence increasing.

When she got up to go, she took the kitten.

"I'll be coming tomorrow with your order from the shop."

Mrs Saunders nodded but then suddenly frowned.

"Make it the day after. I don't need anything, or anybody for that matter, tomorrow."

"But they'll have it all ready at the shop," Annette protested, her heart sinking.

"All right, if you must. But don't come too early." The old lady had reverted to her old brisk manner.

When she set out next morning, the sun was already glowing through brisk white clouds. Annette forgot the uneasy feelings of yesterday and nodded quite cheerfully at Sandy, still working on the hedge.

"Friends yet?"

"Nearly! I'm looking forward to Saturday."

Famous last words!

"Put the things on the table," Mrs Saunders snapped next day. "Give me my list and my bag, will you? There, on the dresser."

All Annette's elation left her like a deflating balloon at the older

Colin Gibson's Almanac

JANUARY

WHEN my daughter was a schoolgirl, I used to take her, two of her chums, and Hamish — our cairn terrier — on a first-footing visit to the lightkeeper's house at Buddon Ness, at the seaward entrance to the Firth of Tay.

There, Charles Liness, the lighthouse-keeper, and Mary Troup, his housekeeper, always gave us a warm welcome.

Charles invited us up to see the top of the lighthouse, and was soon leading the way up and up, and round and round, the spiral stair.

We climbed the metal ladder up to the light itself — massive and immaculately clean and bright.

Charles told us it was a bit creepy up there at nights, especially when birds came fluttering around. When a heavy bird, like an eider, thumped against the glass, it was quite startling.

Down on terra firma again, we had a look at the vegetable garden

Charles's treasures were his carrots — immense in size and pitted under sheets of corrugated-iron. He filled a big basket for us to take home.

"The sma' anes are the best," he said, but I clamoured for some of the "sowsters" — these to put shame on some of the gardeners I knew!

So, sharing our burden, we said our goodbyes and made for home. The lights of Tayport and Broughty Ferry were twinkling, and the dusk was deepening into darkness by the time we reached the noisy streets again.

Buddon Ness Lighthouse.

woman's disapproving tone.

She gave Mrs Saunders the list and bag, and looked desperately round the room, hoping to find a stimulating topic for conversation.

A photo on the dresser caught her eye. Without thinking, she picked it up and examined it while Mrs Saunders counted out change.

"What a very pretty girl! Is she your daughter, Mrs Saunders?"

"Put that down! Who that is, is none of your business! Put it down, I say!"

Annette's hand was shaking as she replaced the photo, shocked by her

15

sharp reprimand.

"You're just like all the others. I don't want to see you again! Do you hear, young woman? Be off!"

Annette didn't wait to be told again. Leaving the money lying on the table, she made a dash for the door and scurried away past the kitchen window.

She was so upset, it was a relief to see Sandy standing in the lane.

"Hello. What's up now?" he asked, astonished to see her tears.

"Sandy! I don't know. I don't know what I've done," she stammered, wiping her eyes self-consciously with a hand.

"It was a photo . . . I was so surprised . . . I'll be all right in a minute." She accepted the handkerchief he offered and mopped her eyes and nose.

Sandy patted her arm soothingly.

"I guess we'll never be bosom friends now," she said at last. "She told me not to come back. I thought we were getting on so well, too . . ." Her voice tailed off.

She suddenly recalled her glance through the kitchen window. Mrs Saunders had been as upset as herself, her hands covering her face . . .

Resolutely, she gave Sandy back his handkerchief.

"I'm going back," she said. "I must. She was crying." Without another word, she returned to the house.

MRS SAUNDERS was sitting as she'd left her, slumped in her chair, her thin shoulders shaking.

"Mrs Saunders — what is it? Can I help?" Annette laid a hand gently on the woman's shoulders.

She stiffened under her hand and, for a moment, Annette felt rigid antagonism. Then the old lady seemed to relax and looked up through her tears.

"She's forty today — it's her birthday . . ."

"It is your daughter, isn't it?"

Ada Saunders clutched the kind young hand.

"Yes — yes. My only one. Forty today. And I've never been in touch — not since she went to Canada.

"She would marry him." She shook her head sadly. "I said he wasn't good enough for her — that she was throwing her life away. But all the time I just didn't want to let her go.

"They married in Canada. Of course, I didn't go to the wedding." She sighed and Annette remained silent, waiting for her to continue.

"She wrote after her honeymoon, but I never answered. And now she doesn't even know where I am! I moved here about ten years ago, you see. I've no-one but her, and I don't make friends easily.

"Well, people don't like me, and that's the truth. And why should they?" Though her voice was defensive, Annette could see the appeal in her eyes.

"Have you any idea what they do in Canada?" she asked kindly.

"I know he was from Toronto and had something to do with television. He was an engineer and they said he was a clever chap."

Annette had been thinking hard.

"I believe I can help. The Canadian Broadcasting Corporation is a much smaller affair than the B.B.C. We could ring up and find out whether your son-in-law is still on their books.

"If he doesn't work for them now, perhaps they'll know where he's moved to. We may strike lucky. Have you got a telephone?"

"Yes. But I doubt, it's too late." Mrs Saunders' face was bleak.

"It's never too late," Annette said firmly.

She walked home briskly that night. Her disappointment over her lost job was forgotten, Ron was forgotten, her bet with Sandy no longer important.

All she could think of was a lonely, heart-broken old woman whom she might be privileged to help . . .

A radiant, Ada Saunders met her at the front gate the next day.

"They rang!" she stammered. "Last night! They rang! They're coming to fetch me." Half-laughing, half-crying, she clutched Annette's arm.

"Would you believe it? Three grandchildren! They've room for me. He's got on well, that lad — they're comfortably off."

"However am I going to manage to pack? I don't know where to begin!" Distracted, delighted, she looked back at the house.

"And it's all your doing. I'll never forget that. Never!" Impulsively, she dropped her crutches and put her arms around Annette.

Annette didn't mind at all that Sandy was waiting for her in the lane later, hoping to give her a lift home.

"It seems it'll be my treat after all," he remarked. And his eyes were warm and kind. □

Christmas Time!

HAS Christmas really spun again
Its special brand of cheer?
With carols, bells and holly wreaths;
The goodwill of the year.

The midnight Mass, the cavalcade
Of greetings, as of yore.
And the star shining up on high,
As of an age before.

The crib, the Babe, the holy words,
The same, but ever new;
Yes, Christmas stays within our hearts
The way we want it to!
— Elizabeth Gozney.

Corbière Lighthouse, Jersey

SITUATED on the south west coast of Jersey, seven miles from the island's capital St Helier, Corbière Lighthouse has been guiding mariners to safety for over a hundred years.

Many locals and holidaymakers alike enjoy the picturesque walk to the Lighthouse, but have to watch out for the tide which can soon cover the causeway and maroon the unwary!

CORBIÈRE, JERSEY : J CAMPBELL KERR

His Flower Girl

by Mary Steward

AS Rob McEwan worked on his allotment, which he'd been doing for many years, he often noticed a little girl stopping to watch. She couldn't have been more than ten and would only stay a few minutes before skipping off, presumably on her way home from school.

His thoughts went back to his own little daughter. She used to come and remind him that his meal was ready and Mum wanted him home . . .

Life was different now. His dear Meg had died some years before, and his son and daughter had married and moved away. They had families of their own now.

His allotment was all he had to fill his days since he retired. And he still got real pleasure, even after all these years, from seeing packets of seeds transformed into crops he could be proud of.

One day the little girl lingered longer than usual. Rob, being near the path, said hello to her. As they talked, he wondered why a girl so young should be interested in vegetables. Few children were . . .

"Why don't you grow flowers?" she asked. "I would if we had a garden."

"Never thought of it, my dear. I do have some flowers in the front garden at home. But those were for my wife, really. I'm more the veg man."

She smiled at him and skipped off.

What a sweet bairn, he thought, and stood leaning on his spade for several minutes after she had disappeared

She'd started him thinking. Why not grow a few flowers, after all?

It was almost the end of the season now, too late for this year. But next year . . . yes, he'd definitely make a plot for growing flowers!

He had some seed catalogues at home, from vegetable specialists. No flowers at all. Ah, well, he could see what he would find at the local garden centres.

He wondered what the other allotment holders would think. "Going a bit soft in the head," they'd probably say to one another.

In spring, after long and helpful deliberations with a very pleasant lady at the local nursery, his small greenhouse was full of carefully tended seed trays.

When summer came, his cronies were surprised. After Rob had got his veg in, he began the meticulous planting out of his precious new plants. Why, they asked, was he suddenly going into flowers?

"Oh, I thought it would make a

Jock Gaffron.

change."

When they pressed him, he would only say that, since his wife died and his family moved away, he'd been hard put to give all the veg away. He just fancied trying his hand at a bit of colour.

They teased him a bit, but he didn't mind. All the time he was remembering the little girl, hoping she'd approve, and enjoy the beauty of the colours.

Strange, he thought, that he hadn't seen her for quite a while. Perhaps she'd gone past when he was busy? Or possibly she'd gone another way home with a friend . . .

But the summer wore on with never a sign of her. Rob began to wonder why.

Surely she hadn't been upset

21

when he'd spoken to her? He'd been careful not to appear too friendly or talkative — though goodness knows, he missed seeing his own grandchildren . . . How often had they been warned about speaking to strangers?

Then, one afternoon, as he was leaving his allotment to go home for a lonely tea, a young woman came walking along.

"What a lovely splash of colour," she remarked. "It really is beautiful. Alison would have loved to see that . . ."

Who was Alison?

Rob thanked the young lady for her kind words, and mentioned, rather shyly, that a little girl had given him the idea of growing flowers. He'd been so disappointed that he hadn't seen her for quite a time.

There were a few seconds of silence, and then the woman smiled.

"I wonder if it was my Alison who told you she loved flowers? She's often said she wished she had a garden.

"She was badly injured in a road accident a few months ago . . ." At his look of horror she rushed on. "She's much better now, but she's lost her sight. Temporarily, we hope. I'm going to fetch her now.

"I'll tell her all about your new garden. I'll try to explain how colourful it is and what it's like — though neither of us will know the names of the flowers!"

HOW sad Rob felt after she left. Could this really be that happy little girl who had been his inspiration? And now she might never see what he had created . . .

Some days went by before he saw mother and daughter coming along. They stopped to speak to him.

"Hello, Alison," Rob said gently. He found it hard to keep his voice steady for, sure enough, this was the little lass who'd changed his mind about flowers.

He asked her if she would like to touch them, and as mother and daughter walked carefully amongst the blooms, Rob was deftly picking a large bunch. He watched Alison hold it to her face, and his heart swelled.

"Thank you, Mr McEwan," she said softly. "I'm going to come and see you again."

"I hope so, m'dear," Rob said gruffly.

Next year, he thought as he waved goodbye to Alison and her mum, I'll have to grow flowers which have a lovely scent. He could only think of stocks and tobacco plants, but he was sure the helpful lady at the nursery would know.

She was so nice, she'd evidently spent her entire working life with plants and flowers, and Rob had felt quite at ease with her.

Yes, she'd know all right, and it wouldn't be any hardship to go and talk to her. He still didn't know her name, though he'd heard someone call her Molly. A nice name, he thought, for a nice lady.

Going soft in the head, was he? Well, perhaps, but if so, it was a nice feeling — he'd recommend it to anybody! □

HOWEVER smart Kirsty's navy suit was, it was definitely not waterproof! Just as she thought the rain couldn't get any heavier, the deluge increased until its noise blanked out any other.

Experience should have prepared her for the wait — after all, she had hung around for Doug in all weathers. But, enough was enough and, ducking her head, she stepped from the doorway to scurry back to work through the downpour. The bank would, at least, be warm and dry.

"Kirsty! Kir-stee!"

Kirsty halted, refusing to turn round. Doug had finally arrived.

Breathless, comfortable and dry in his hiking jacket, he bounded into her path.

"I'm late," he pointed out unnecessarily. "Look at the state of you!" And he laughed, blue eyes peering mischievously at her.

Kirsty glared at him through the drips which ran steadily from her dark hair on to her jacket. Her narrow skirt was clinging to her legs and she shivered.

Majken Thorsen.

Doug pretended to wring the water from her hair. Kirsty jerked her head away.

"That's enough!" she snapped, unwilling to be joked out of her irritation.

"I'm in this state because I've just spent three-quarters of my lunch-hour in a doorway — in the pouring rain!" Her voice was wavering with cold.

Opposites Attract ...

by Sue Moorcroft

Indignation fuelled her aggravation and she barged past him.

"If this is the best you can do," she muttered, "we might as well call it a day."

"Cool down!"

Doug grinned uncertainly, realising his suggestion was unwise.

"I'm sorry I'm late — again. I couldn't help it. There was someone in the shop and I couldn't close up. I'm here now."

Avoiding his comforting arm, Kirsty wiped her face with a trembling hand.

"I'm going back to work."

"Be reasonable," he protested. "You could've brought an umbrella — or waited inside."

Kirsty swung round sharply.

"If the rain had started before I left, I would have put on my coat!" No matter how much she hunched her shoulders, the chilly water still found its way down her neck.

"And I couldn't have waited inside the café without ordering!"

She resumed her angry march.

"If you can't make the effort to keep to an arrangement occasionally, just forget it," she flung over her shoulder. "Forget it! Forget me, and forget our relationship!"

This time, Doug let her go. But he stared after her slight, wet figure weaving through the people as the rain bounced about his ankles.

K IRSTY hung her jacket on the corner of the radiator by her desk. She was serious and dedicated to her job, efficient and confident. Funny then that she should have got involved with someone so disorganised, who scrambled through life perpetually late for appointments. The attraction of opposites, she supposed.

One evening last summer, while between boyfriends, she'd allowed a colleague to persuade her into a foursome. The other couple had edged away to the other end of the noisy, town centre club — not really Kirsty's sort of place — and left her with Julian, her blind date.

Kirsty remembered Julian vividly. He'd been full of his own self-importance and clearly liked the sound of his own voice. She'd first noticed Doug when she'd turned her head to stifle a yawn.

He was engaged in a little pantomime immediately behind Julian's solid back. Appearing to listen intently to the conversation, he gradually allowed his eyes to glaze and lids to droop. After a moment he jerked, as if waking up.

Kirsty tried to resist a grin. Doug glanced at his watch and then at Kirsty and pulled an agonised and outraged face.

Kirsty looked away and then looked back. Julian had just interrupted his monologue to replenish their drinks at the bar.

"Quick!" A long, brown hand closed around Kirsty's. "It may be our only chance!"

Allowing herself to be pulled along, giggling like a child, Kirsty

Colin Gibson's Almanac
February

ON a bright frosty February day, Arbroath's Keptie Pond ("The Lochie") presents an animated scene.

Like many a young Arbroathian, I learned to skate there — using my father's "skeleton" skates. They were far too long for me, and had a habit of dropping off! But if my artistic skill on the ice didn't amount to much, at least I had lots of fun.

The Water Tower on Keptie Hill made a wonderful backdrop. Even today, visitors look admiringly at this hilltop fort, and wonder about its history.

Well, they might be surprised to learn it was built at the end of the 19th century — to hide two water storage tanks! The builders — no doubt inspired by Patrick Allen Fraser of Hospitalfield, who had an eye for romantic buildings — obviously went to town. They constructed a fairyland castle in what could be called Scots baronial style.

Massive battlements with gargoyles projecting, loop-holes, and buttresses, deeply-recessed windows and door, and a watch-tower turret, all feature. Between the main building and the retaining wall is a fine promenade 10 feet wide, commanding a view not only of the town itself, but of the coast, the Angus countryside and the distant Grampians.

As it turned out, the output of the well at Noet Loan, and the storage-tanks, proved insufficient for the town's needs. So, eventually, a more adequate supply was brought by pipe-line from the clear-running Noran Water in North Angus.

The Water Tower became redundant. But Keptie Hill wouldn't be the same without its hill-fort. It is the high-note in a wonderfully attractive part of the town.

Keptie Pond, Arbroath.

somehow found herself running hand-in-hand down the street. Then through the carpark into West Gardens, where the air was heavy with the scent of new-mown grass, to collapse panting on a bench.

"You poor thing!" Doug laughed, eyes alight. "What have you done to deserve him?"

Such crazy behaviour was normal from Doug, Kirsty soon discovered. In contrast to her staid job at the bank, he sold secondhand records and tapes from a small shop which attracted all sorts. He found people infinitely entertaining and cultivated an enormous circle of acquaintances.

Kind and unorthodox, Doug might wade into the pond to rescue a duck, or snooze in the cinema if he was tired. He would carry the shopping of an old lady who looked worn out, or stop to offer a stranger help with a broken-down vehicle.

Unfortunately, he was incapable of watching the clock.

Kirsty's working schedule was clearly defined. She was entitled to an hour for lunch — when she took it. She began work at 8.45 a.m. each day, including two Saturday mornings each month.

She was part of a holiday rota and wore a suit to work. It suited her organised nature.

Doug opened the shop after he'd had breakfast, looked at the paper and sauntered to town. If he had customers he'd stay open, if not, he might close.

He took lunch when the shop was quiet and if he felt like a holiday, he'd take one. Doug didn't own a suit.

It was beginning to look as if we were too incompatible, Kirsty thought drearily, before turning her attention to the ringing of the telephone on her desk.

IT'S me." Doug's voice echoed in her ear. "Are we still friends?"
Kirsty sighed and tried not to sound petulant.

"Maybe we're too different, Doug. You can't be bothered with punctuality — I can't be bothered to wait for you to get round to me."

"I had customers," he pointed out gently. "I was talking to this young guy . . ."

"That's the kind of difference I mean!" Kirsty declared frostily. "You forget . . . you forget I'm waiting, you forget I only get an hour for lunch!"

"I'm sorry," he said quietly, tempted to tell her that just maybe she was too organised, and unwilling to compromise.

"How about a test case?" he suggested brightly. "I'll meet you at three o'clock . . . absolutely, positively three o'clock . . . on Sunday afternoon by the big tree. The students are putting on a theatre in the park."

Kirsty wavered, they both liked the theatre and regularly supported both students and local amateur societies.

"If I'm late, I'll eat sour apples," Doug coaxed, causing Kirsty to grin and agree.

It was funny how long Saturday seemed, spent alone. Usually, she spent the day in Doug's cosy shop among the racks of records and tapes, while Doug, dressed in jeans and one of his enormous collection of T-shirts, chatted to the colourful customers.

And later they'd go on into the evening together, to a quiet pub or a noisy club, on long walks, bike rides, or parties. Doug liked to try everything once.

Kirsty found this solitary evening the longest part of a long day. And, she realised, it led to a long night as the clocks were to change to British Summer Time. Carefully, she reset her watch, two clocks and the video timer before going to bed.

Waking to a bright day, Kirsty spent a lonely morning getting ready to meet Doug.

The neighbourhood park was filled with fathers and children; most likely taking advantage of the extra hour, she thought. Would Doug's good resolutions last until three o'clock?

Doug was there, waiting patiently, crouched at the base of a tree.

Strolling past the bandstand towards him, Kirsty was surprised to see the park was emptying. Where was the students' theatre?

Doug looked inexplicably glum. She couldn't recall seeing him look anything but cheerful and lively before.

"Are you OK?" She stood before him.

He looked up at her before rising.

"Have I been taught a lesson?" he replied evenly. "I suppose I asked for it. And, if it makes you feel better, I admit I didn't enjoy it."

"Didn't enjoy . . . ?"

"Waiting two hours for you."

"We said three o'clock!" Kirsty glanced at her watch.

"And now it's five."

"Five?" Kirsty said uncomprehendingly, her mind racing.

Doug let her see his own watch, then swung Kirsty round and pointed to the black and gold clock on the tower across the road.

They both read five o'clock.

Her face flushed, Kirsty slowly turned back. She had difficulty in raising her eyes to his.

"Did the clocks go back, or forward?" she whispered.

"Forward."

"I put mine back."

A silence grew whilst Kirsty inspected Doug's baseball boots and Doug looked at the top of Kirsty's head.

"Back?"

"Back. I got it the wrong way round, I suppose."

Doug tossed his head back and began to laugh. He laughed until he had to hold on to Kirsty's shoulders, and then the tree, for support.

"How wonderful!" he gasped. "You finally got something wrong!"

She had to join in, to laugh at her own ridiculous self.

"It's something I've always had a block about," she confessed. "I can't always remember which is which."

"Spring forward, fall back," he managed, striving for breath. "Put your clock forward in spring, back in autumn or 'fall'."

"Oh." Kirsty was crestfallen. "What a fool I am."

Thinking of the recent, boring, two-hour wait he'd endured, Doug suddenly pulled her into his arms.

"I think we both are," he remarked. □

The Reluctant Babysitter

Y OU did!"

"I didn't! I'm telling Gran!"

Footsteps thundered, voices shrieked. Geoffrey struggled to concentrate on his paper. It wasn't that he minded Eileen's grandchildren, he told himself, he just wished they weren't so loud.

He sighed.

The trouble was he just wasn't used to them. He and Margaret had never had children and, though sometimes they'd thought it might have been nice, they'd been fine as they were.

They'd always been very happy and the best of friends. Then Margaret had died, suddenly and heartbreakingly, almost five years ago now.

by Sally Bray

Mark Roberts.

Those had been hard days — he'd missed her so much. For months, he'd simply drifted, lost.

If it hadn't been for his sister, he might have grieved forever. Somehow, she'd convinced him that he had to go on living, that he owed it to Margaret to be the happy man she'd known. So, slowly, he'd returned to the world.

Then he'd met Eileen. Eileen, with her laughing smile and loving nature; gentle, widowed Eileen, who understood as no-one else did.

They'd become friends and she'd invited him home to the sprawling house she shared with her dogs and cats.

Geoffrey, too, loved animals and that bond had brought them closer still. Friendship had grown into love. Soon they'd known they wanted to spend the rest of their lives together.

It might have been perfect, except that Eileen's first marriage hadn't been childless. Eileen had a daughter, Joanne.

Joanne wasn't a problem. He liked her and she seemed to like him. But she had two children of her own — and as they lived nearby, they were for ever popping in.

He didn't dislike Kitty and Ben, he just didn't understand them. He had no idea how to talk to them, how to treat them.

He'd never dealt with children before and he felt he was too old to start. Their noise was too much for him, and their chatter, and their terrifying modern toys.

It seemed to be mutual. They fell warily silent the minute they saw him and side-stepped round him, as if they thought he might explode. This perturbed him most of all. .

"They don't hate you," Eileen explained patiently. "They're scared of you, that's all."

"Scared of me?" Geoffrey echoed, genuinely distressed. "What am I, some kind of ogre?"

"No, of course not!" Eileen smiled. "But they're not used to you, and you're not used to them. You just have to get to know each other, that's all . . ."

But months had passed and nothing had changed.

He wanted it to. He wanted to love them, and be their friend — for everyone's sake, but, above all, for Eileen. He loved her so much and they were her family.

Maybe, he thought without much hope, he'd get on better with the new baby. Joanne was expecting a third child soon and things were bound to be different then. The baby wouldn't need to get used to him; it would accept him as part of its life.

T HEN Joanne was taken to hospital with sudden complications. The children came to stay with their grandmother.

"You don't mind, do you, love?" Eileen pleaded.

"Scott would look after them at home, but, with work and everything, he just can't. And neither he nor Jo need any more worry now. I'll make sure they don't bother you —"

What a monster she makes me sound, he thought miserably. And what a monster I probably seem.

"Of course I don't mind, love," he said gently. "You bring them, they'll be fine. You never know," he went on with frenzied optimism, "it might make all the difference . . ."

It hadn't.

Eileen did her best. Most days she took the children out while, with barely-concealed relief, Geoffrey stayed at home to mind the animals.

That Saturday, Kitty and Ben were tired when they returned and Eileen put them to bed. She was coming downstairs when the phone rang.

"It's all right, love, I'll answer it."

Geoffrey heard Eileen's voice change as she spoke into the phone.

Suddenly anxious, he went to her side.

"Yes . . . yes."

Geoffrey stood, barely breathing, at the sight of Eileen's face.

At last, she put down the phone.

"That was Scott . . ." She bit her lip. "The baby's on its way. Jo wants me —"

"Oh, love . . . Will it — be all right? It's early, isn't it —?" He cursed silently. If there was a wrong thing to say, he was sure to say it . . .

"Five weeks early." Eileen blinked back tears. "It's not critical, it's not too early, but . . .

"Oh, Geoff. If anything happens — it'll never be the same . . ."

"Now that's enough," Geoffrey said very gently. "Nothing's going to happen. You go to them. They need you and you need them. You'll feel better once you've seen Joanne.

"And don't worry. It's going to be all right."

She managed a smile.

"You make me believe it," she said unsteadily.

"Good. Now go on, off you go."

"Thanks, love." She hurried to the door, then stopped abruptly.

"The children! I can't —"

"Don't worry about them, either," Geoffrey said rashly. "I'll look after them!"

She looked at him lovingly for a moment.

"What would I do without you?" And then she was gone. The door slammed behind her and Geoffrey heard an uncertain voice from upstairs.

G RAN?" It was Kitty. "Grandma, Gran —"
His heart plunged. Slowly, he made his way upstairs. Sitting bolt upright in bed, Kitty glared at him suspiciously.

"I want Gran!"

"She's not here," Geoffrey answered, lightly. "I'm afraid you'll have to settle for me. Now, what's the trouble?" The words fell like rocks.

"I want a drink of water . . ." Kitty's bottom lip trembled.

He left the room; filled a glass; brought it back; set it down.

"Anything else?" He hadn't meant to sound blunt.

"Can I get you anything else?" he amended, more softly.

"No," Kitty murmured warily. "Thank you." She sipped delicately, then lowered the glass and stared at it.

Geoffrey wondered whether to stay or leave. As usual, he hadn't a clue.

"Where's Gran?" Kitty looked up. "You said she wasn't here. Where is she?"

"She's out." He was on solid ground there. Or thought he was.

"She can't be." Kitty shot him down. "She wouldn't go out and leave us. She never goes out and leaves us. Where is she really?"

What have you done with her, was the unspoken accusation.

His heart sank. No doubt Eileen would have thought of some gentle explanation, but all he could think of was the truth.

"She's gone to the hospital," he told her leadenly. "To be with your mum while . . . she has your little brother or sister."

The child looked up in alarm.

"Does that mean Mummy's ill again?" she asked, and his heart twisted at the fear in her eyes. "Is she —?"

"No, love." He spoke instinctively. "No, love, no!"

He sat down on the bed.

"It just means the baby's going to be a bit early, that's all," he said gently. "Some babies don't like waiting. Just like we don't," he quipped, but Kitty wasn't listening.

"I don't want another rotten brother," she muttered fiercely. "The one I've got's bad enough. I'd rather have a sister. Only I don't really care as long as —" She broke off.

Wretchedly helpless, Geoffrey squeezed her hand.

"Why don't you come downstairs for a bit?" he suggested. "Have a snack, watch television — whatever you like. Anything's better than lying here worrying.

"Besides, I'd like some company. It's lonely without your gran."

He smiled and, after a second's pause, she smiled back.

"Come on then!"

As she scrambled out of bed. Ben woke up and stared sleepily.

"What's happening?" he murmured.

"We're going downstairs for a bit," Geoffrey said easily. "Just for a chat, till your gran gets back. Want to come?"

"Yeah!" Hurling himself out of bed, he was halfway down the stairs before the others had reached the door.

"You know," Geoffrey said amiably, as he followed with Kitty, "my sister once thought I was a rotten little brother, too. In fact, she probably still does."

Kitty stopped in her tracks.

"You've got a sister?" She seemed stunned at the idea.

"Oh, yes. Three years older. Very bossy. But we like each other really. Just like you and Ben do, even if you fight."

"I didn't really mean he was rotten." Kitty bit her lip. "Sometimes he's

Tyndrum, Perthshire

FIVE miles north of Crianlarich, settled in a glacial valley, you'll find Tyndrum. This is a popular stopping-off place for travellers heading north to Glencoe, west to Oban, or south towards Loch Lomond. Yet there is plenty of great scenery to draw tourists to Tyndrum itself.

Walkers enjoying the famous West Highland Way pass through on the route from Milngavie near Glasgow to Fort William, and no doubt welcome the chance of rest and refreshment in this bustling village.

These days, gold mining nearby has led many to believe that the area could be about to experience a "gold rush"!

TYNDRUM, PERTHSHIRE : J CAMPBELL KERR

nice. It's just . . ." Tears welled up in her eyes.

"Is my mum going to be all right?" she pleaded. "I'm scared . . ."

"She's with people who'll take good care of her," Geoffrey said gently. "They look after people like her every day. Don't worry, love."

She didn't speak, but he saw the trust in her eyes. Wordlessly, she slipped her hand into his and they walked downstairs.

He was grateful for her silence because he wasn't sure he could speak for the lump she'd brought to his throat.

Ben danced impatiently at the foot of the stairs.

"What were you talking about?" he demanded.

Kitty recovered.

"Nothing you'd understand," she told him cuttingly. "You're just a baby." And, safe at Geoffrey's side, she swept grandly past him.

Geoffrey winked at Ben and was rewarded with a grin.

The rest of the evening passed in a haze of orange juice, chocolate biscuits, and board games.

"You mustn't let us win," Kitty ordered. "Especially Ben. It's bad for him because he's a baby. I like winning properly."

And she did, repeatedly. It was all rather fun. He'd never realised before that children could actually make him laugh, and felt a bittersweet regret for what might have been . . .

But with Kitty and Ben he still had time. He could talk to them now, play with them, get to know them. It wouldn't be so hard. If only nothing went wrong — if only their mother was all right . . .

He hadn't felt like this since he'd known he was losing Margaret. He hadn't known then that he'd one day find Eileen, find her family, become a part of her world. He hadn't known how much he'd love them, how much he'd care — hadn't known they'd become his family, too.

The children grew tired and fell asleep, warmly snuggled on the sofa.

The night crept on. Midnight passed and a new day began. The world was still, so still.

He wondered whether Eileen would phone or come home. What was happening?

At last, he heard the door and, heart hammering, he rushed from the room.

EILEEN was there, tears on her cheeks — yet she was smiling. "Geoff. Geoff, it's all right. She's had a little girl, a girl called Annie. She's tiny but she's perfect and oh, Geoff, it's all right . . ."

"Oh, love —" Heart soaring, he swept her into his arms. "Oh, love, that's wonderful —"

"Another granddaughter." Eileen laughed. "Oh, I can't wait to tell Kitty and Ben —"

Kitty and Ben. Geoff started guiltily — they were still in the sitting-room.

"I think," he said slowly, "you can tell them now." Looking round, he saw them behind him.

Curious, wary, fearful, hopeful.

Eileen smiled.

"You've got a baby sister. What d'you think of that? Your mum's fine, and you've got a new sister —"

"A sister?" Kitty was entranced.

Ben was disgusted.

"A sister? You mean the baby's a girl —?"

"It's better than a boy," Kitty snapped. "And it's two against one now, so you just watch it."

Geoffrey laughed.

"Never mind, Ben, you've still got your dad. You'll manage."

"We'll all manage," Eileen said contentedly. "And now let's get you back to bed. Whatever are you doing up, anyway?"

"We've been up all night," Ben boasted.

"Grandad let us stay up," Kitty explained. "Grandad let us come downstairs. He brought us down, 'cause I was scared."

"Grandad . . . ?"

Eileen turned slowly towards him, eyes wondering.

He felt crazily close to tears.

"Well," he said, "I'm a sort of grandad, aren't I?"

"You're a lovely one." Eileen kissed him. She said no more, but she didn't need to. Kitty had said it all.

He was one of the family at last. □

Fortune

*A*S I fold away her day clothes
    And retrieve her tiny shoes,
I am storing precious memories
    My heart will never lose. . .

As I pick up all her toys,
    Some broken during play,
I am gathering the treasures
    Of another lovely day.

Out there, in the garden,
    Lies her battered pail and spade,
And funny broken castles
    That her tiny hands have made.

Oh, some may count their fortunes
    In coins made of gold —
But mine lies in the wonder
    Two baby arms can hold!
                                    — Marjorie Blackmore.

A Stranger To The Island

by Betty McInnes

THOSE passengers who weren't in too much of a rush to catch the evening ferry spared a curious glance at the elderly lady standing on the quay.

She seemed out of place somehow. For one thing, she was dressed in an outfit more suited to city streets than the chilly conditions prevailing in the Pentland Firth. Thick jackets and mufflers were more usual here.

The wind was whipping froth from white horses, and the evening was so dull and murky, lights were lit early.

She didn't board the little ferry when the bustle of departure began, but continued to stand aside quietly, staring raptly across the water. She gazed out to the island, just visible through the gloom — a dark hump of land rising out of the sea.

The ferry passengers settled down thankfully in the saloon, out of the cold. One or two idly contemplated the slim, elegant figure on the quayside as the ferry pulled away from the shore.

She has a nice face, that old lady, they thought, as the memorable features faded into darkness. She must have been bonny when she was young. Still was! That sort of beauty does not fade with age.

Nothing had changed, Emily thought, as she watched the ferry leave for the outer islands. You could still see eight lights from this vantage point — and the loom of a ninth, far out beyond the skerries.

Once, she could have named all the lighthouses flashing a warning to shipping navigating the treacherous firth, but now a few eluded her. It was so many years since she had last stood on this spot.

She had travelled so far away . . . always moving on, stopping a while, making good friends, leaving them behind. A busy, restless, exciting life. Over, now.

Looking out across the firth, it was obvious that the island itself had changed. There was darkness where once small, friendly lights had glowed in many houses. Now it was uninhabited — the last family had left last year, she had discovered.

The island lighthouse still functioned and she held her breath as a pattern of light swept out across the restless water. Six flashes in quick succession. Could she ever forget?

Emily leaned against the old stone wall forming part of the breakwater, sheltering from a keen east wind.

How troubled I was, the last time I stood here, she recalled — and just as unsuitably clad. I was just nineteen years old!

* * * *

How out of place a young city girl must have seemed to the fishermen working on the quay. She remembered she'd been wearing a summery blouse, stylish full-skirted costume and the daintiest of Edinburgh shoes — a far cry from the local women's clothes.

In those far off days, tourists were rare and she was treated with amused curiosity. Yet the kindly fishermen were gentlemen and treated her with courtesy.

It had been a bearded elderly man who had approached Emily, eyeing her shoes, his brows raised.

"You want to cross to the island, miss? Well, Harold here is the island boatman, and his boat is the *Alpha*, out there." He indicated a burly fisherman and a broad-beamed rowing boat bobbing close by.

Emily looked at both nervously. Neither compared favourably with the steam ferryboats and efficient crews plying to and fro across the Forth.

"Isn't the boat rather small?" she ventured.

"No, no, miss!" Harold protested in shocked tones. "It's not small at all. This boat will transport eight islanders — or four trussed ewes. Indeed, you'll not find a finer craft from here to the skerries."

There was a chorus of agreement from the others.

"I only want to make a very short visit to the island, returning this afternoon. Would that be possible?" she asked nervously.

"No trouble at all." He beamed. "It's fortunate that I have a bag of meal to deliver to the island store — and a coop of white Leghorns to Malky Jamieson, not to mention letters —"

"How much will the trip cost?" she interrupted cannily.

As a shop assistant working in a fashionable Edinburgh store, she could command comfortable wages. But she seemed to have spent a fortune already — travelling from Edinburgh to Wick and then on to this out-of-the-way spot.

A heavy silence fell and all eyes were on Harold. He cleared his throat.

"One shilling, single. Two shillings for a quick return. First class, sitting in the bows."

"That's robbery!" she cried in shock.

He looked insulted.

"Well, indeed it would be robbery if it was just a wee sail you were making across a millpond. But that's the North Sea out there."

"Aye." Another man nodded. "There's nothing but currents and whirlpools and hidden rocks. Two shillings is a small price to pay."

Emily knew it'd do her no good to argue — she had no choice.

"Very well." She sighed, glaring at Harold. "But you won't see a penny until I'm back here — safe and sound."

"That's a reasonable bargain," Harold agreed, hauling on the ropes which brought the *Alpha* in to the side of the quay.

After Harold had been rowing steadily for ten minutes, Emily became anxious.

"I said I wanted to go to the island, you know!" They were heading in the opposite direction, towards very choppy water.

"Just so." He glanced over one shoulder and gave a hefty pull on the portside oar. The boat smartly turned into a dangerous-looking tidal race. He settled back contentedly to ride the rapids while Emily gritted her teeth and clung on.

"This'll take us directly to the slipway at the south end, miss.

Colin Gibson's Almanac

March

THERE were three of us — my daughter, her school chum, and myself.

With a north-west wind ruffling the Firth of Tay, and a promise of milder weather in the air, we intended to follow the cliff-top path from Wormit to Balmerino. It's a north Fife coastal route of many ups and downs, exposed in places, but mainly sheltered by whins and thickets of sloe or blackthorn.

It takes little more than an hour to reach "Ba'murnie," but it's picturesque all the way — especially near the salmon fishers' bothy.

The salmon fishers' bothy.

Balmerino village is old and quaint — white cottages, red pantiled roofs, farm steadings against the foreshore. But many come here to visit the ruined Cistercian Abbey which looks over a wide vista of firth and finely wooded shore.

The Abbey is 13th century and, in its heyday, several Scottish queens sojourned here. The saintly Ermengarde, widow of William the Lion, attended the Abbey's foundation and grew to love this quiet sanctuary. Madeleine, queen of James V, came here to recuperate after illness. And on a cold but bright March day, Mary, Queen of Scots arrived — youthful and happy then.

We had a look at an ancient Spanish chestnut tree in the Abbey grounds. This is "Queen Ermengarde's tree," planted by her well over 700 years ago.

We noticed the immense layered boughs and gnarled trunk, which I calculated to be about 24 feet round.

Old though it was, already the branches and twigs were budded anew, and hundreds of yellow aconites made of the grass around it a royal carpet of gold.

"It has been a good journey," he said a little later, "considering the dangerous state of the tide."

"You didn't warn me!"

"Ah well, I could see you were troubled . . ." He eyed her sympathetically. "I'm not a man to pry, but is it a young man?"

Emily hesitated before she spoke.

"Yes," she answered, with a deep sigh. "It is a young man."

39

THE very first time Emily had noticed Murdo Macdonald, he was dressed in naval uniform. He stood outside the high-class city store one morning, taking a keen interest in a display of ladies' hats, while she and the other shop assistants arrived for work.

There was an excited little flutter amongst the girls. Handsome young naval officers were common enough in the busy port of Leith, but somewhat scarce in Edinburgh's Princes Street.

"He was in gent's outfitting yesterday — buying winter socks," Emily's friend, Rose, hissed in her ear. "In May!"

"Maybe he's heading for the Arctic." She laughed, hoping he wasn't. He was a very handsome young man . . .

At the sound of her laughter, he turned, looked straight into her eyes, and smiled. Her emotions, which she'd hardly been aware of in the past, were suddenly thrown into confusion.

She walked on in a daze, into the staff quarters to put on her pretty apron. She automatically held out her hands for inspection for ragnails, which might catch on fine materials, then walked dreamily through the store to her work station.

The manageress believed in rotating staff, so that each assistant gained experience in all departments. Emily was serving on the perfumery counter this month.

The young sailor walked in, bold as brass, when the shop opened at nine. He stopped at Emily's counter and her heart jumped. But his words soon brought her back down to earth.

"I'd like to buy scent for my young lady."

She might have known that he'd have a sweetheart somewhere. Emily pinned a smile on her face, hiding her disappointment.

"Had you anything special in mind, sir?"

"Something cool, flowery — and fresh as a warm breeze blowing across heather."

She blinked in surprise.

"We — we have a lovely perfume called White Heather."

"That's lucky, isn't it?" He grinned.

"Yes, it is."

"I'll take a bottle of lucky White Heather."

Lucky for someone else, she thought, as she carefully wrapped the crystal scent bottle. He paid the staggering price and took the gift, which he immediately handed back to her with a grin.

"For you, ma'am!"

And that was the start of a whirlwind courtship. He had ten days' leave, he told Emily. Such a short time to fall in love — but that's what happened.

They met every day, and she discovered he looked every bit as handsome in civilian clothes. They ate a quick lunch of tea and sandwiches, bought from a vendor in Princes Street gardens. They spent a leisurely evening together after the shop closed.

A Stranger To The Island

Emily took Murdo home to meet her widowed mother, who was just as charmed.

They walked together hand-in-hand every day, and sometimes, discreetly, they kissed, knowing that time was short.

"To think that if I hadn't gone into the shop that day to buy socks, I would never have seen you. I'd never have met you, never have known you were the only girl for me," he marvelled, as they walked together on the leafy crags of Corstorphine Hill.

"Winter socks in May, Rose tells me!" She laughed. "I suppose you need them on board ship, heading for the Arctic."

He stared in astonishment.

"What do you mean, dear girl? The only ship I ever board is the *Pharos*, the lighthouse ship. And I steer well clear of the Arctic, I can tell you!

"I'm a lighthouse keeper, Emily, and need thick socks to keep my feet warm when I'm on watch. No heating up in the lantern room, you know, in case the glass steams up and dims the light."

"But — but your uniform — I assumed you were a ship's officer!" Emily was amazed.

He smiled in amusement.

"It's very similar." Then his smile faded as he caught sight of her expression.

"Emily, does it make a difference?"

She couldn't look at him in her distress. Of course, it made a difference!

Lighthouse keepers were sent to outlandish places — the back of beyond, the end of the world . . . cliffs, rocks, seabirds, mountainous seas pounding the shore! And their wives were expected to go with them, to share isolation and loneliness!

"I'm a city girl, Murdo!" she cried in distress, feeling as if her heart must break.

He took her in his arms.

"I know, but you must know by now how much I love you. I want to marry you." His voice was tender. "My leave is up tomorrow. Think about my proposal, my dear little city girl. Write to me, tell me if you will become my wife . . ."

BUT she couldn't put down on paper what she had to say to Murdo Macdonald today, Emily thought.

Harold's boat scraped against a rough stone breakwater, rousing her from her thoughts.

"We're here," he announced.

"Here" was a scatter of stone cottages, seemingly built at random on the hillside, all basking in sunshine. "This is the south end of the island — warm as Monte Carlo, but without the gambling. The minister wouldn't approve of that!" Harold joked as he helped her out.

A Hillwalker's Dream

TO start in the early morning
  When the mist is on the ben,
And the sound of the curlew calling
  Stirs echoes along the glen,
And the feel of the springy heather
  Is balm to your booted feet,
And the windless summer weather
  Promises later heat —

To rest in a sheltered hollow
  At noon, on a sun-drenched height,
With your thoughts set free to follow
  The eagle in her flight —
To gaze on the crags below you
  Where a puff of cloud lies curled;
Absorb all the mountains show you,
  And feel that you own the world!

And then, in the purple gloaming,
  When the sea flames in the west,
To turn your thoughts from roaming
  To the peace of home and rest;
Content in the sun's spent radiance,
  Trudge happily down the brae,
And leave the hills to their silence —
  Your friends for another day.
              — *Brenda G. Macrow.*

Ron Weir.

Her skirt trailed in the sea, her fancy shoes soaked by a wave.

"And the north end, where the lighthouse is?" she asked.

He gave her a speculative glance.

"It's all cliffs there, with a north-east wind, and the sea thundering in, sending spray higher in the air than an Edinboro' fountain!" He winked.

"I'm thinking you must be Murdo Macdonald's young lady," he ventured and a pink flush tinged her cheeks. "The island has been agog to see you. He's a very fine young man, Murdo." He nodded.

"Well, if it's to the lighthouse you're wanting, old Jimsie will take you along the road, rather than your shoes."

Old Jimsie was as weathered and weatherbeaten as ancient mahogany. He had a horse-drawn cart, made from an ancient lorry chassis. He settled

The Cuillin from Elgol, Skye.

Emily comfortably on the leather passenger seat.

The road stretched before them — one mile long, straight as a ruler. The lighthouse buildings ahead gleamed white in the sunlight.

She almost turned and fled. What was she going to say to Murdo?

"You'll be Murdo Macdonald's young lady," old Jimsie said.

"How did you know?"

"This is a friendly island, and Murdo Macdonald is a fine young man. We've all been waiting to meet you." He gave her a welcoming grin.

A merry crowd of youngsters, just released from a little school on the breast of the brae, suddenly surrounded the cart, yelling and cheering.

She waved and smiled breathlessly until they were left behind.

A knot of rosy-cheeked women, gathered outside the store for a blether, turned and shouted a welcome as she passed.

"Yes," she agreed quietly, "I can see it's a friendly island."

Harold had described the north end of the island well. The cliffs rose high and sheer where the lighthouse stood, and the north-east wind tangled her tidy hair.

She could hear the sea roaring below the cliffs, sending spray skywards, in a rainbow mist that drifted across the road and tasted salty upon her lips.

Suddenly there was Murdo, standing before her, the wind ruffling his hair, a paintbrush in hand. He dropped it with a clatter and held out his arms.

"Emily, dearest. What are you doing here?" His voice was anxious but there was joy on his face.

"What I have to say could not be written in a letter, Murdo dear," she said quietly.

* * * *

A hand touched Emily's shoulder, bringing her back to the present with a start.

The night had grown colder and darker as she stood there with her memories. She could no longer see the island, except when the beam of light shone out.

Her husband put an arm around her shoulders.

"Satisfied now?" he asked gently.

She smiled up at him.

"Yes. I just wanted to stand here one last time."

"Why here? Why not May Island, Ardnamurchan Point, Kyleakin, Mull of Galloway, Dunbar — all those other lighthouse stations where we lived and loved and were so happy?"

"Because —"

"Don't tell me!" Murdo Macdonald said triumphantly. "It's because this island is where you agreed to marry me — even though you were a city girl."

"Yes, Murdo. I'm a romantic old woman."

His dark hair was pure white now, and she reached up and kissed his dear face fondly. It felt cold to the touch in the north-east wind.

He would never know that she had gone to the island that day to tell him a city girl could never marry a lighthouse keeper . . . But, true love, and that friendly island, had changed her mind. And she had had no regrets.

Murdo linked an arm through Emily's and they walked slowly back to the car.

A long journey home lay ahead, but at the end of it was the cosy little retirement bungalow that was their pride and joy. It was just below Corstorphine hill — in the heart of the city! □

Mike Heslop.

**by
Christine
McKerrell**

"YES, YOU CAN!"

H ARRIET peered short-sightedly into the dressing-table mirror,
retrieved a stray curl and anchored it firmly in place. Today of
all days she had to look her best.

In the bedroom opposite, Jenny would be almost ready. Harriet
pictured her granddaughter, blonde hair framing a heart-shaped face,
black gown hanging neatly on her slim, young frame.

She and Jim were so proud of her. A "first" in combined sciences —

who would have thought it?

Harriet remembered the letter arriving as though it were yesterday. She'd been so excited, almost more so than Jenny herself, and couldn't wait to share the news with her friend, Marjorie.

Marjorie Ellis lived just across the street. She wasn't far off eighty, and these days was pretty much housebound. Harriet had got into the habit of popping in every day for a chat.

Over a cup of tea, she produced Jenny's letter of acceptance from the university, handing it to Marjorie with undisguised pride.

"It's exactly what she wanted," she told her friend, and Marjorie nodded.

"You'll be glad she opted for Denton, rather than somewhere further afield."

Harriet shrugged.

"She could have gone to any one of half a dozen places, but, yes, I am glad she'll be close to home. Her grant will go further, for one thing!"

Marjorie nodded shrewdly.

"And you'll be able to keep an eye on her, of course." Her eyes twinkled, and Harriet coloured slightly. She knew she was sometimes a little over protective of Jenny, but hadn't realised it was so obvious.

"Oh, that doesn't come into it," she said hastily. "Jenny's a sensible girl. I've no worries on that score." She sighed.

"I just wish I'd had her chances. I'd have given anything to go to university."

Marjorie placed her cup and saucer carefully on the small table at her side.

"And why don't you?" she said after a moment or two.

"Oh!" Harriet smiled. "There were so many reasons. Money was tight in those days. Then, of course, I met Jim, and it wasn't long before the children came along."

"No," Marjorie said. "You weren't listening. I asked why don't you, not why didn't you."

Harriet gazed at her in amazement.

"Oh! I couldn't, not now. I'm too old, and anyway you need all these qualifications to get in," she ended lamely.

"Excuses, excuses." Marjorie Ellis tutted. "Nowadays anyone who wants can do it. It's no longer a privilege, you know, it's a right!" She chuckled. "And you've got certificates, haven't you? You told me so."

* * * *

Yes, Harriet thought ruefully, she had certificates all right, but to think of doing anything with them at her age, well, it was ridiculous, wasn't it?

Almost as ridiculous as wanting to be a ballet dancer when she was ten! Well, her mother had soon put paid to that idea.

"Don't be silly, our Harriet," she'd said in her no-nonsense way. "You're too old to start now, and, anyway, you're not very light on your feet, are you, dear?"

Even at ten, Harriet had accepted the truth of that remark.

"If it's dancing you want —" her mother continued, with barely a pause in the seam she was running up on her old treadle machine "— there's a group meets in the church hall on Saturday mornings."

"But that's country dancing!" young Harriet protested.

"And more use to you by far. Mark my words. A bit of country dancing never goes amiss at weddings and socials."

Her mother had been right, of course, but it was a long time before Harriet stopped dreaming of frothy white tutus and satin slippers. It seemed there was always a grown-up who knew best lurking in the background.

TAKE school, for instance. Harriet had always had a notion for science. Harriet Jenner, Nobel Prize Winner! It was a favourite daydream, guaranteed to get her nicely through two periods of maths followed by double geography.

Miss Allen, her form mistress, had blanched visibly when Harriet suggested she might like to take physics and chemistry in third year.

"But your maths, my dear!" She'd sighed. "I really think you should stick with what you're good at — history, home economics. You'll thank me for it in the end."

And Harriet supposed she had, really. Well, she'd got a pass in history, hadn't she? And cooking was a kind of science . . .

She'd thought about university, of course, but Harriet wasn't making excuses when she'd told Marjorie Ellis that money had been tight in the Jenner household. And anyway, as the career officer said, with her qualifications, technical college and good basic office skills were her best bet.

Harriet had done well. She'd been offered a job with an insurance company almost as soon as her college course finished. And she would most likely have gone far if she hadn't met Jim, who worked for the same company.

They were married within six months and, though Jim wasn't one to insist on a wife's place being in the home, Paul's birth, almost a year to the day after the wedding, rather decided matters. Working mums had been a bit of a rarity back then.

The twins, Sandra and Lilian, followed soon after. Jim was ecstatic and Harriet was pretty contented with her lot. Jim was a good husband, and the children were no worse than any others and a sight better than many.

They made a lovely family. Everyone said so. Harriet knew more than one of her less fortunate friends would readily have swapped places. Of course, she'd been happy!

Paul went away to university in due course, but most weekends he turned up with a rucksack of dirty washing and an appetite sharpened by a week of his own cooking. He graduated with honours, to Harriet and Jim's delight, then promptly took a job in Brussels.

Mary's

**by
John Taylor**

It was Tuesday when Mary rang and we were not leaving till mid-morning on the Friday. So you can guess what Anne did.

"Can't go empty handed, John," she said. Despite the fact that Mary would make a spread for us, Anne made a banana loaf, a gingerbread, some "fly cemeteries" (fruit slices) and, blow me, boiled a piece of brisket!

"Be nice cold with a salad, John."

Bless Anne, she's more for giving than taking.

We were in for a fine time with our Mary and Tom.

After lunch on the Saturday, Tom and I took a run up Glen Lyon whilst Mary and Anne went shopping in Perth.

On Sunday morning we attended the service at their wee church.

After a great Sunday lunch, when Anne and Tom were looking at some sheep and lambs, Mary took me down their garden.

WHEN I came in for my breakfast the other morning, I could see by the beam on Anne's face that she was feeling pleased with herself.

"John, our Mary wants to know if we would like to go to spend this weekend with them."

By Anne's face, I knew we were going.

To be honest, I was pleased, too.

Lambing time was over for another year and I think we both felt a few days rest away from the farm would do us good.

I am fortunate — I can get away knowing that the sheep and lambs will be well looked after.

Letters and postcards arrived regularly at first — he was a bit homesick, Harriet could tell, and she would reply at great length. No-one else in the family had time to add more than a postscript, not with the busy lives they all led. But Paul soon settled in and the letters gradually tailed off.

By the time Sandra went to the local college, the days of "good basic office skills" were gone. It seemed there was something for everyone now. Computer studies . . . aromatherapy . . . iridology!

Sandra had never had the time or the inclination to settle down. She was too busy sailing the oceans of the world, managing a beauty salon on a cruise liner.

Special Silver Birch

It's a beautiful garden.

She stopped at a tall silver birch.

"How old do you think that tree is, Dad?"

"It's thirty-seven years old, dear."

She gave my arm a squeeze and said, "Good for you."

I'LL tell you how I was so certain about its age. Here's its history.

We were over the moon when we learned our daughter was expecting. It didn't seem long before we got a call from Mary to say Tom was taking her to hospital as she had pains.

"Tom will give you a ring, Mum, as soon as we know anything."

I could tell Anne was on edge, waiting for the phone to ring.

One o'clock, two o'clock. I came in from the fields at about three. No ring. Poor Anne was going out of her mind.

Just before six, the phone rang.

Anne picked it up.

"Hello, Mum - false alarm."

Anne really let off steam.

"Mary, why didn't you ring before? Dad and I have been out of our minds with worry."

The Farmer And His Wife

"Sorry, Mum. . ." There followed a long story as to why she hadn't been able to phone.

The hospital had suggested she should go home and come back when the pains got bad. They thought that would be in about a week's time.

They had left the hospital and gone for a wee walk. Then Tom had taken Mary out for a high tea, whilst we were waiting for that telephone call!

It was a beautiful afternoon so they had gone for a walk in one of the many forests in their area.

By the side of the forest, a small self-set silver birch was growing. It was about four feet high. As it would have just been broken down when the machines came in to fell the trees, they carefully lifted it and took it home.

That night they planted it in their garden, to commemorate the birth of their first child, who did arrive a week later.

I know their son is now thirty-six. That's why I could easily remember the tree's age.

I've always thought ever since, if everybody planted a tree for their first-born, what a difference it would make to the world.

Lilian was a real home body. No-one was surprised when, at eighteen, she married her childhood sweetheart and, in due course, presented Harriet and Jim with their first grandchild. They called her Jenny, after no-one in particular, and she was the most perfect baby ever, in Harriet and Jim's opinion at least.

Certainly no baby was more loved. But even a new grandchild didn't fill the gap in Harriet's life. Days seemed interminably long, as Jim left home soon after eight and was seldom home before six.

He was doing splendidly at work, had an office of his own and a secretary, no less, and they had no money worries.

When the local paper ran an article about university places for mature students, it seemed to Harriet that she might at last realise some of those buried ambitions.

She mentioned it to her friend Bella the next evening as they drove in through the gates of the high school.

Harriet and Bella had met at night school. Together they had moulded intransigent clay into lopsided pots, struggled with the intricacies of conversational German and moaned through innumerable aerobics routines. Bella was a good sort, only a year or two older than Harriet.

When Harriet mentioned the newspaper advert, Bella groaned.

"Go back to school! What, old fogies like us? Face it, love, we're past all that."

Harriet had buried her regrets in the pedal bin next morning along with the potato peelings, wrapped up in the local paper.

She didn't feel over the hill. She was still the right side of forty, after all, but of course it was ridiculous.

Bella was right. Maybe she should get a little job. Perhaps one of the charity shops in the High Street would welcome some help.

The call that put an end to all such thoughts came at teatime. Harriet had just taken a steak-and-kidney pie out of the oven when the phone rang, and Jim rose with a resigned sigh.

When he came back into the kitchen his face was ashen and he seemed to have aged ten years.

The lorry driver wasn't to blame, the inquest said. His brakes had failed for no apparent reason, but Lilian and her husband had been killed outright. Baby Jenny, strapped into the back seat, escaped without a scratch.

The first few months were difficult. Harriet and Jim had forgotten just how demanding a baby could be but, little by little, a routine that suited all three was established.

AND now Jenny was off to university, a BSc majoring in chemistry, no less! Where had the years gone? Harriet folded the letter back into its envelope with a smile.

"She's such a clever girl." Her voice was full of pride.

"There's nothing wrong with your brain," her friend said softly.

"Oh, I couldn't possibly do anything like that," she insisted, shaking her head.

"My dear, it doesn't do to go through life putting yourself down." Marjorie smiled.

In the warmth of the summer morning, a bumble-bee had found its way in at the half-open window and buzzed angrily against the glass.

"We shall have to let it out." Marjorie peered up at it as Harriet opened the window as far as it would go. They watched in satisfaction as the insect rose heavily into the warm air.

"There." Harriet smiled. "It's a shame to see them trapped."

"Everything needs to fly free at least once in its life," Marjorie said.

Harriet threw a suspicious look at her friend, but Marjorie's face gave nothing away.

"Did you know," she went on, "that the bumble-bee is aerodynamically unsound?"

"I'm sorry?"

"Technically they can't fly."

"But that's . . ." Harriet stared at her.

"Silly? Yes." Marjorie nodded. "Especially when we've just seen evidence to the contrary."

"Then how —?" Harriet frowned.

"Well!" There was an unmistakable glint in Marjorie's eye. "Perhaps nobody told the bumble-bee."

Harriet smiled into her mirror. She doubted if she would ever qualify for the Nobel Prize now, but there were other goals just as precious.

She nodded to herself, and there was a defiant tilt to her head.

"If the bumble-bee can do it, why not me?"

She was just pinning her favourite brooch on to the lapel of her best suit when Jenny burst in, her pretty face flushed with excitement.

"Gran, can you do something with this cowl thing? It won't lie flat whatever I try."

"Here, give it to me." Harriet shook her head fondly.

Jenny nudged her slyly.

"Practice for next year," she teased and Harriet cast her eyes ceilingwards.

"If I ever get there!" She groaned, and finished straightening out her granddaughter's robes.

"Here, let me look at you." She stood back. "Jenny, you look lovely. Your mum and dad would have been so proud of you."

Jenny threw her arms round her.

"Proud of you, too, Gran. Who would have thought it? My gran the student!"

"Away with you. I'm just playing at it!" Harriet protested.

"Nonsense. You're loving every minute. Grandad and I can't wait to see you up on that platform next year!"

"Maybe." Harriet shook her head. "Miracles have been known to happen." She picked up her handbag from the bed. "Come away, now. Grandad's waiting to take some photographs before we go."

"Seriously, Gran," Jenny persisted, "you'll have deserved it. It takes a lot of courage to do what you're doing."

"Not courage, love. Determination maybe. Ignorance certainly!" Harriet chuckled, remembering a warm summer's day and an angry insect buzzing against a window pane.

"Ignorance?" Jenny said, bemused, and Harriet smiled as she led the way downstairs.

"Tell me, Jenny," she asked, "did anyone ever expain to you about bumble-bees?" □

The Colour

by Margaret Gilmour

S HE was a lovely old lady, wasn't she? We'll all miss her."

Across the line, Katrina could hear emotion in her father's voice as clearly as though he had been in the next room instead of hundreds of miles away.

"Mind you, she had a good innings," Dad went on. "She was well over ninety, you know. Born at the turn of the century, like the Queen Mother, though she would never admit to it.

"Effie was quite a character, eh?"

Katrina smiled. You couldn't help smiling when you thought of Great-Aunt Euphemia. Effie had a sharp sense of humour and never hesitated to speak her mind.

She'd never married. There had been a sweetheart once, but the mud of Flanders had claimed him.

"If the Good Lord saw fit to take my Angus for himself, he must have meant me for other things," she would say, with her own brand of resignation.

Katrina's mind went winging back to the happy times spent with Effie in the tiny, whitewashed cottage overlooking the bay. There were always a few brown hens scratching in the yard, a velvet-eyed cow in the field and, at the side of the house, a tight brown stack of peat piled ready for the fire.

How many years had it been since she had savoured the fragrant smell of a peat fire? That would always bring back Effie and summer holidays — the tang of the sea, and unmistakable reek of peat-fire smoke. Nothing in the world could match the magic aroma.

"She's left something for each one of you children, you know. Your cousin Joan is to have her collection of Coronation plates, and Robert gets the grandfather clock.

"You were always her favourite, though, Kat. She used to say you reminded her of herself when she was a wee girl.

"She wanted you to have that picture you always liked. Do you remember it? The one with the daisies?"

"The daisy picture! Oh, yes! Dad, did she really?" Katrina's eyes filled with tears.

For as long as she could remember, the daisy picture had hung in pride of place, halfway between the parlour door and an old pine dresser, where Effie lovingly displayed her treasured plates and mugs.

"Do you know, Dad, I can shut my eyes and see every detail of that painting even now."

Of Love

The canvas showed a window half draped by a filmy web of lace, and a cloudless sky beyond. On the window-ledge stood an earthenware jug full of marguerites, their bright starry faces turned to the light.

The contrast of colours — the deep terracotta vase, soft green leaves and the bright gold discs in the centre of the flowers — gave the picture a vitality that had never failed to fascinate Katrina.

The artist had painted a lacy shadow on some of the upturned flower faces and across the painted sill, a shadow that somehow gave the entire picture an aura of mystery.

During those wonderful holiday times, if the rain had lasted for days and the whole world seemed damp and dreary, Katrina had only to look at the daisy picture, and suddenly it was summer again.

A memory came unbidden to her mind. She had slipped into the parlour while her aunt was feeding the hens, and was busy tracing the shadows with her fingers when Effie found her there.

"Now, lassie. What are you up to in here? Ye ken fine the parlour's only for the Sabbath." The voice was firm, but there was no anger in Effie's wise old eyes. "Just wanted to see the daisy picture, eh? You like it, don't you, lass?"

"I think it's lovely." Then, with the innocence of the young, she had added, "Can I have it, please, when you're dead?"

Effie had laughed at the child's bluntness, and promised. And now that day had arrived, and with it the knowledge that Effie had gone.

"So, I'll wrap it up well and send it on to you." Her father's voice interrupted her thoughts.

"Thanks, Dad. I'd be grateful if you would. I just wish I'd made more of an effort to go and see her over the last few years. But you know how things were, with Stephen and everything . . .

"Look, Dad, will you get some flowers for me? Something white would be nice. Small, but pretty. If you can arrange it, I'll send some money on."

"'Course I will, love. I'll see to it straightaway, and take them with me when I go. The funeral's tomorrow and I'm driving back to Ullapool this afternoon for the ferry." He paused.

"Look, dear. About Stephen. Isn't it time you were getting over that now? It's been years since he left. I hope you're not still moping!"

"Of course not — don't worry about me. I've made lots of friends here. I don't even think about Stephen any more," she lied.

KATRINA put down the receiver and faced herself in the hall mirror. Why had she told her father Stephen meant nothing to her now? How could she forget him?

When he had first told her of the wonderful job he had been offered in the States, Katrina had assumed they would simply bring the wedding forward. It had been quite a shock to realise he wanted to postpone everything until he got back.

"It would be difficult, Kat. We wouldn't be able to settle anywhere . . .

54

Colin Gibson's Almanac
April

I WAS in my post-diploma year at the School of Art in Aberdeen when, one April morning, I was called down to the Head's room.

I laid aside my palette and brushes, and answered the summons. There I was introduced to a distinguished-looking gentleman who had come from Balmoral Castle. He wanted me to come and paint the deer.

At first I had visions of myself becoming another Landseer. But no! The deer to be painted were ornamental stags placed here and there in the Castle grounds. Apparently, the King wanted them painted in their natural colours.

So, as soon as I was ready, I was driven, complete with painting kit, to Balmoral. Here I found the Castle in the hands of painters and decorators, and not a Royal (except for the ornamental stags) in sight.

First, I walked around to see what I'd have to do. The deer were life-size, made of cast iron, each one set on a stone pedestal with a little prickly hedge surrounding it.

These hedges presented difficulties, but I soon learned how to surmount them. With my palette and brushes in one hand, this left the other free to clutch an antler and retain balance.

Well, speak of realism! I gave these stags the full treatment — the flashing eyes, the red nostrils, the grass-stained teeth, the red-russet coats.

It took me a week to complete them, and I still had to paint a dainty deer in the middle of a fountain. I wasn't at all sure what it was, but I took it to be an Alpine chamois. So, as soon as the gardener laid planks across and made it accessible, a chamois it became!

A delightful week! The weather was good, and Deeside full of early April's promise of spring.

Ornamental stag, Balmoral.

I'll be on the move all the time. And it's only for a year," Stephen had pleaded. "I'll be back before you know it."

But one year had led to another, and Stephen's letters became less frequent and less loving. Finally came the words she'd been dreading. The engagement was off.

He hated having to hurt her, he said, but he had met someone else . . .

Katrina smiled wryly as she recalled the last line of that letter.

55

You'll soon find another man, he had written. *Somebody who really deserves a nice girl like you.*

So he had only ever seen her as a nice girl. He had drifted into the engagement because it had been what she, and everyone else, expected of him.

She'd tried to convince herself she was glad he'd found someone he really cared about, but the rejection had cut deep.

She couldn't bear the sympathy in her friends' eyes. When an opportunity arose to transfer from Edinburgh to head office, she had jumped at the chance of living in London.

For a while she'd concentrated on working her way up the ladder and soon made new friends among her colleagues.

But Stephen was still in her heart and mind, and she wasn't going to take the risk of being hurt again. Sensing Katrina's detachment, young men soon lost interest.

The most recent, John, had been persistent. Then, a moment that might have blossomed into romance had slipped past before she realised it, and he was gone.

Since then she'd become restless. She was twenty-nine years old, living alone, and becoming increasingly aware that something was missing from her life.

The picture arrived just a few days after the phone call from her father. Katrina carefully untied the knotted string and smoothed the outer layers of wrapping paper to use again.

"Aunt Effie would approve of thriftiness," she said aloud, smiled to herself at the thought. Then, unable to wait a moment longer, she tore off the final wrapper.

The frame was peeling slightly, but it was nothing that couldn't be put right, she thought.

The daisy picture itself looked just as she remembered. Perhaps the colours were less bright, but the magic had not faded. She still loved it and was delighted to have it.

Katrina hugged the canvas to her breast, and breathed a silent thank-you to Effie's memory.

* * * *

"That's a nice painting. Did you buy it here? It would look lovely in my lounge, wouldn't it?"

Katrina gave her friend Anthea a warning look.

"I didn't buy it. And before you ask, the answer is no, you can't have it! It's my inheritance from Aunt Effie. I did tell you about it." Katrina shook her head in mock despair.

"Can't you climb down from 'cloud nine' for a moment or two and remember us mere mortals?"

Anthea and her David were soon to be married, and for months every conversation tended to be dominated by details of the wedding.

Reception, guest lists, flowers, fabrics and fittings — the list seemed endless. The fact Anthea had actually noticed the picture at all came as quite a surprise.

"I remember now," Anthea was saying. "It's the one you liked when you were a kid, isn't it? You're right, it is rather nice, though the frame is a bit tatty.

"You're quite sure you don't want to part with it? It would brighten up the corner of my lounge, and if I bought yellow curtains . . ."

"No way. It's mine and it's staying!" Katrina was determined to steer her friend away from the subject of home furnishings.

"I was wondering about having it valued. Do you think it might be worth something?"

"Don't ask me. I'm no expert." Anthea laughed. "But I know a man who is!

"Alistair Fenton. You know, the Fenton Gallery? We were at school together." She smiled reminiscently.

"He was crazy about my sister Vicki for years. He even wanted to marry her at one stage!"

Katrina wasn't surprised. Any man would have wanted to marry Vicki, a stunningly beautiful girl. When she and Anthea were fourteen, Katrina had longed to be Vicki.

"So why didn't he marry her? What went wrong?"

"Oh, she dumped him after a while. She said he was too ordinary and boring!"

Katrina's heart immediately went out to Alistair Fenton. She knew only too well how he felt.

"So — you think Alistair Fenton might look at my picture?"

"I'm sure he would. Even if it's not some long-lost 'old master', he could at least sort out a better frame. He does all sorts of restoration work, you know, as well as valuations.

"Tell you what, why don't we drop in on him at the gallery? Then afterwards we could have a look at bathroom fittings in Harrods!" she added with a wicked glint in her eye.

H ERE we are!" Anthea stopped outside a large double-fronted shop. A few select oils and watercolours were tastefully arranged in the bow windows. Above was the simple gold-leaf legend, *Alistair Fenton — Fine Arts.*

Suddenly Katrina felt nervous. Her precious painting, in its cheap brown paper wrapping, seemed insignificant compared to this artistic perfection.

"Perhaps we should forget about it. This place looks very grand . . ." She hesitated on the doorstep.

"We've come this far, so let's get on with it. No backing out now! Besides, I haven't seen Alistair for ages. He'll be glad to help."

Inside, a tall man rose from his high-backed chair, a lean finger marking a place in the book he still held, as though reluctant to be disturbed. Alistair Fenton was slim and dark, and very tall. He was dressed surprisingly casually.

At first he looked forbidding, but when he saw Anthea his eyes lit up, and he hurried forward to wrap her in a bear hug.

Katrina, looking on, could only think how absolutely mad Vicki must have been to turn down such a gorgeous man. He didn't look at all boring to her. In fact, she was thinking how striking he looked when he turned his head and caught her eye.

He smiled, and his whole face changed. Katrina was drawn to him instantly.

* * * *

That evening Katrina answered the door and was surprised and delighted to find Alistair Fenton on the step.

"I hope you don't mind my calling," he said. "I got your address from Anthea, and I thought I'd return your picture myself." He paused.

"Besides," he added, "it's given me an excuse to see you again."

Katrina's heart gave an unexpected flutter.

"Come in," she said. "It's nice to see you."

"And you've no idea who the artist is?" he asked a few moments later while Katrina was making coffee.

"It's a pity. It is charming, and beautifully executed, but I hope you're not expecting to make a

Loch Rannoch.

Lakeside

BY cool still waters near the old house
  I sit in peaceful muse,
Taking in the solitude
  Of sweeping lawns and views.

Lakeside trees are turning gold,
  To herald autumn's reign;
Only darker evergreens
  In wintertime remain.

Up into a cloudless sky,
  A flash of sapphire wings,
And somewhere in a treetop near
  A blackbird sweetly sings.

A little moorhen splashes
  Along the water's edge,
A downy duck is preening
  On a sunlit ledge.

Reflections on the water
  Rippled by the breeze;
A squirrel hides his store away
  Before the winter freeze.

Calmly, gently, softly
  The lakeside soothes all pain,
Its beauty fills my soul with hope
  For I am home again.
                    — *Enid Pearson.*

Dennis Hardley.

fortune at the Antiques Roadshow! I doubt if it would fetch more than a few hundred pounds — perhaps a little more at auction."

"Oh no, I don't want to sell it," Katrina broke in hastily. "I just wondered about the value."

Alistair moistened a corner of his hankie and rubbed gently at a painted petal.

"Look at that," he said, showing her. "I don't suppose you realised it was so dirty. Proper cleaning would bring out the true colours and let us appreciate the shadow effect to the full. It would give it a new lease of life.

"I'd be happy to undertake the work, if you would like me to."

"Thank you, I'd be delighted. Perhaps you could do something about the frame at the same time?"

Alistair nodded.

"Will it take very long?"

"Not long, but I do have quite a backlog at the moment. I could have it ready for the fourteenth, if that's OK."

"Oh, that would be fine." Katrina frowned. "That date sounds familiar. Oh — that's the day Anthea and David are getting married!"

"I know. I'm looking forward to it."

"You're going to the wedding?" Katrina looked at him. "But Vicki will be there! Won't you mind?"

It was out before she'd thought, and she stood there, horrified at herself.

"Why on earth should I mind?" He was smiling at her.

"It was — just something Anthea said," Katrina faltered. "It's not important."

"And what was Anthea been saying? That I loved Vicki and wanted to marry her?"

Katrina nodded, looking away. But Alistair reached out and tilted her chin, forcing her to meet his steady gaze.

"It's true," he admitted. "I thought she was the love of my life." Then she saw a smile twitch at the corner of his mouth.

"What Anthea omitted to tell you was that it was a very long time ago. In fact, we were both seven years old!"

Suddenly Katrina felt light headed — and light hearted, too.

"So now you know!" Alistair grinned. "What do you think? Shall we go to the wedding together? Unless, of course, there's someone . . .?" He paused.

Katrina looked over his shoulder at the painting. Its colours, its contrasts, brought the usual lift to her heart. She looked at Alistair, and smiled.

The smile was enough. Next moment she was in his arms.

"There's no-one else," she whispered, against his shoulder, and the daisies, as bright as if Alistair had already cleaned them, seemed to nod their approval behind him. □

A Cry For Help

by Fiona Curnow

Antico.

OH, no, Joan thought, as she gritted her teeth. Not again. Not now. The baby's high-pitched wail shattered her peace — just when she'd been settling down to listen to that concert on the radio she'd been looking forward to.

Joan sighed as she glanced at the colour photographs lining the kitchen wall between her and the baby's screams. This time she'd have to say something; she really would. She'd have to go next door to complain.

Before she had a chance to change her mind, Joan bustled down her garden path, and up to the neighbouring front door.

What was she to say, exactly? She'd barely swapped a dozen words with the young couple who'd moved in six months before. She knew the wife's name was Lucy — the assistant at the village shop had told her — but that was about all.

She surprised herself with the forcefulness of her knock.

AFTER a few moments of silence, she'd just started to convince herself that this was a bad idea, and was about to walk away, when the door clicked open.

The words of reproach died on her lips.

Lucy was cradling her baby against her shoulder, her eyes heavy and red — the tears obviously just wiped away. She was wearing her dressing-gown, yet it was a quarter to two in the afternoon.

"Hello," she said quietly. It didn't sound like a greeting, so much as a tentative cry for help. "Would you like to come in?"

Joan followed her inside, feeling rather taken aback.

This isn't what I'd planned, she thought. I've already missed five minutes of that concert. What am I going to say?

She glanced into the kitchen as Lucy led her through the hall. The lay-out was a mirror image of her own cottage, but there the resemblance stopped. There was a huge pile of washing-up beside the sink. On the table was an onion that had only been half chopped.

Joan cleared her throat. She had to say something.

"The baby . . ." she began, "is — um . . .?" She saw the anxiety on the other woman's face and tried to speak gently. "Is she all right?"

Lucy bit her lip and the baby started grizzling again.

"Oh, I wish I knew. Every time I put her down, she starts crying. I can't seem to do anything but feed her, wind her, change her, feed her again." Her own gaze flickered guiltily towards the open kitchen door.

"It's not normally like that," she continued self-consciously. "But we've eaten everything out of the freezer now. I've got to make something for our tea — it's not fair to expect Greg to do it all when he comes home from work. But she just won't let me."

She juggled the baby awkwardly, trying to quieten her.

"And the health visitor's due at half-past. I haven't even managed to get dressed," she finished in a rush.

Joan smiled wryly. It had been — how many years? But that helplessness in Lucy's eyes . . . It was suddenly all coming back to her.

"What were you trying to make?" she demanded briskly.

"Just spaghetti bolognese — nothing terribly ambitious."

"Well, I think I can manage that." Joan surprised herself. "You sit down and see to her."

It was strange, cooking in a kitchen so like, and yet so unlike, her own. And it was strange, too, to think she was cooking for someone other than herself again.

Why had she offered? An impulse, a memory? Joan couldn't quite say.

As far a cookware went, young Lucy seemed to have the best of everything. She found herself enjoying the sharpness of the knives, the newness of the pans.

She even found a radio and managed to catch the last half-hour of her concert while she worked.

Once she'd got the bolognese underway, Joan went back through to the lounge. The baby was still wide awake on Lucy's knee, but quiet now. There was a brand-new, expensive-looking Moses basket on the floor.

"I know what you're thinking," Lucy began. "But if I put her down in it she'll scream."

There was a baby care book open on the floor and Lucy quoted from it in a mocking voice.

"A newborn baby will sleep for around sixteen hours a day! Yes, but they don't tell you that for most of the time, she'll want to sleep on you!"

Joan sat down beside her, smiling sympathetically.

"How old is she now?"

"Three weeks."

"And what have you called her?"

"Grace."

"Grace." She was surprised. "Funny how all the old names are coming back.

"She's such a little scrap, isn't she?"

Lucy's shoulders had begun to relax but now Joan saw them tense again.

"Little? Do you think so? I wish I could be sure she's getting enough," she said worriedly. "I mean, she wants to feed and feed and feed, and the book says —"

"She can't read yet. Never mind the book. She'll tell you what she needs. Didn't you say the health visitor was coming soon? That'll put your mind at rest.

"Come on, give her to me while you go and get yourself sorted."

Lucy handed her baby over, looking relieved but a little guilty, too. Then she hurried upstairs, and Joan soon heard the sound of a shower running.

JOAN took her first really good look at Grace and smiled. To think that if it weren't for this little person, she wouldn't have been sitting here in the first place.

Grace looked back with dark, dark eyes that seemed to take in everything.

Joan touched her cheek against the baby's — it was so soft. And she smelled so sweet . . .

She hugged baby Grace — she felt lovely. It was so much nicer to hold a real baby than sigh over snapshots —

She realised Grace was sleeping at last and laid her down in the Moses basket, keeping a hand on her little, rounded tummy for several minutes, until she was sure she wasn't going to wake.

Without turning, she knew that Lucy had come back into the room.

"How did you manage that?" the girl whispered.

"My guess is that you try to put her down the second her eyes close. Don't rush it. Make sure she's sound asleep. After all, she was part of you for a long, long time. She's not used to being alone in this big world."

"I'm a hopeless mother, aren't I?" Lucy sat down beside her, sighing.

"Not at all," Joan said with feeling. "Just new to the job."

They sat and watched Grace sleeping for a while. Eventually, Lucy spoke.

"Don't they look beautiful like that?"

"They have to — it's their insurance policy. Otherwise we'd leave them on the nearest doorstep and run!"

Lucy turned to her, a strange kind of hope in her eyes. "You too?"

"Oh, I was just the same with my boy at first." She chuckled. "Thirty years ago — well, thirty-one.

"He's got two little ones of his own now," she answered Lucy's unspoken question. "They live in Vancouver and send me pictures regularly — at least every couple of months."

They were both quiet for a moment.

"I'm sorry if her crying disturbs you," Lucy said quietly.

"It's OK."

"No, really — that was why you came round, wasn't it? I could see it in your face."

Joan suddenly felt a little ashamed.

"Well, all right then, it was," she admitted. "But we were all Grace's age once — I'm as guilty of forgetting that as anyone."

They looked at each other and there was real gratitude in Lucy's eyes. But before she could say anything, there was a knock at the front door.

"Oh no, the health visitor! Just when you'd got her off to sleep, too."

Joan laid a hand gently on Lucy's arm, trying to calm her.

"We got her off once — we can do it again."

The health visitor made it awkwardly through the door with her black bag and set of scales.

"I'll just go and make us a cup of tea, shall I?"

Joan took her time in the kitchen. It wasn't, she felt, her place to intrude. Lucy was obviously on edge.

By the time she'd checked the bolognese, made the tea and carried the tray back into the lounge, the health visitor had all but finished.

"No," Joan heard her say, "she's exactly average for her age. A bonny little thing. Just remember, she won't be that tiny for long. Enjoy her."

Lucy picked Grace up, and held her fiercely against her shoulder. She swallowed hard and closed her eyes for a moment — obviously fighting back relieved tears.

Finally, she began to rock backwards and forwards very slowly, singing Grace an old, old song Joan hadn't realised people of her age still knew.

Colin Gibson's Almanac

May

FROM Fettercairn, in Kincardineshire, my road took me to the Clatterin' Brig — the starting point of two hill tracks. One road leads into the Glen of Drumtochty, and the other to the famous Cairn o' Mount and then on up Glen Dye towards Deeside. In doing so, it climbs from 400 feet to 1400 feet in the space of two miles!

I was heading for Drumtochty as I had an invitation from Mr Langlands to visit Drumtochty Castle. At that time, the castle was a boys' boarding school and Mr Langlands the headmaster.

When I arrived, I was given a warm welcome, not only by Mr and Mrs Langlands and the teaching staff, but also by their boys and their pets. These included a very stately Irish deerhound, a jackdaw which flew down from the battlements and landed on a boy's head when he tinkled a little bell, and Rusty, an amiable spaniel.

Rusty, the spaniel.

I saw the classes at work and then, after lunch with the whole school in the former ballroom of the castle, the headmaster took me to see the art department, housed in the church hall, near the entrance gates.

Most of the paintings were class rather than individual efforts, and took the form of murals in poster-colour — exciting and happy efforts.

I was particularly taken with one painted mainly in sandstone reds, clay greys and so on, which showed mammoths, dinosaurs, reindeer, footprints of early man, and prehistoric birds and fish.

It was a subtitled, "Painted by I.B. using the materials of Stone Age". Certainly a saving on paint, and very cleverly done!

As the baby sagged against her mother's neck, Joan suddenly felt like an outsider. She moved to open the front door for the health visitor.

The other woman smiled conspiratorially at her.

"I'll tell you now," she whispered, "we were worried about Lucy there for a while. But it must make such a difference having her family around." She smiled. "I expect you were just the same when she was tiny.

"See you next week."

She can't think I'm Lucy's mother, Joan realised, and bridled for a moment. Then she felt a lump rise in her throat as she thought about the cold, flat photographs waiting for her on the kitchen wall — and the welcome in Lucy's grateful eyes.

There was no point in putting the woman straight, just yet . . . ☐

Over The Hills Far Away

LET'S do something different this weekend." Lilian Marshall looked up from her knitting and immediately recognised the faintly restless look on her husband's face. She knew that look only too well. She'd seen it quite a lot lately and found it disturbing.

She had a sudden image of their next door neighbour, Frank Nelson. Only a year younger than Bill, Frank had gone around wearing that same restless look for months before he ran off with his twenty-four year old secretary!

"Different?" she asked warily. "What exactly do you mean by 'different'?

"And don't suggest camping. I absolutely refuse to spend a single night under canvas! Not after last time. I've never been so uncomfortable in my entire life."

"I know, but that was only because it was a bit wet."

"A bit wet! It never stopped raining for three days and we were washed away in the middle of the night when the river burst its banks. Everything got soaked and . . ."

"All right, all right. I know it didn't work out but it could be different this time. The forecast is quite good."

"No. Camping is out. If you want a change, why don't we just book into a hotel somewhere? Or perhaps we could try one of those specialist weekends, painting, or wine appreciation, or . . ."

...ll And

by Jan Whitfield

"Good heavens, Lil, don't you understand? I want something to *do*. It's spring. We should be thinking of some activity to get us going again after winter, not sitting in some stuffy hotel like a couple of old fogies."

Lilian's heart sank. Every word confirmed what she had suspected for months.

Bill was bored, bored with his life. With her? He was fifty-three, nearly a year younger than herself, and if you believed everything you read, he was at a dangerous age.

An article in a magazine had recently caught her eye about how to deal with what the writer called the mid-life crisis in men.

At one time, she would have skimmed through the article and joked with Bill about it later. But since reading it she found herself watching her husband closely, convinced that she could see many of the danger signs . . .

Lilian sneaked another look across the hearth and saw him fidgeting.

She bit her lip and tried to focus her mind on the knitting, but the intricate twists and knots of the Fair Isle pattern seemed as complicated and confusing as her thoughts, and she found it impossible to concentrate.

Suddenly Bill shot bolt upright in his chair and smacked his balled fist into his other palm with a triumphant shout.

"I know! A bike!"

"A bike? You mean cycling?" she gasped and dropped several stitches. "You must be joking."

"I've never been more serious, Lil. You used to love cycling. Remember the old tandem?"

"But that was more than thirty years ago! I haven't been on a bike since the boys were little. I've probably forgotten how to do it."

"Nonsense. You can't forget. It's like swimming or . . . or riding a bike!" He grinned like a boy. "Let's forget we're grandparents for once. They say you're only as old as you feel. Well, I feel like a teenager, so why not?"

I knew it, thought Lilian. He resents his age and his responsibilities, just as it said in that article.

What was it the writer had advised? *Don't let him think of you and his family as a millstone. Make a determined effort to keep your relationship as fresh and interesting as possible.*

"But cycling? We couldn't. What would the neighbours think — and the children?"

"Who cares what they think! Oh, come on, Lil, don't be such a stick in the mud!"

Her mind was racing but she struggled to keep her voice calm as she stammered, "But, Bill, cycling? I couldn't."

"Don't be so negative, Lil. You're always going on about not getting enough exercise and fresh air. This would be an ideal opportunity for us to do both. It'll be wonderful!"

Working out at the club and playing squash twice a week had kept Bill trim and muscular. Lilian thought of the cellulite on her hips and thighs

Mother's Day

JUST a bunch of daisies,
* Clutched in a small boy's fist,*
Just a pair of shining eyes,
* As blue as love-in-a-mist,*
Just a hug, a home-made card
* With wobbly words, to say:*
"I Love You, Mum" — that was enough
* For me, on Mother's Day. . .*
Enough to make my whole day glad
* Were those small tokens from my lad!*

And now, so many years have passed,
* My little boy has grown*
Into a tall and upright man,
* With children of his own.*
But still he never does forget
* To come, on Mother's Day,*
With chocolates, expensive card,
* And beautiful bouquet.*
Such lavish gifts, so why do I
* Look back down the years, and sigh. . .*

For that wee, harum-scarum chap,
* Bright-eyed beneath his bobble-cap,*
Who thrust wild daisies in my lap?
                    — Kathleen O'Farrell.

and groaned inwardly.

"But . . ." Lilian tried desperately to think of a halfway reasonable excuse. "I think Tony and Jill want me to look after little Susie this weekend."

"You're always looking after Susie." Bill drew his brows together. "I agree our granddaughter is an absolute darling but I don't see why you have to give her all your spare time."

She thought of the article again.

Don't let middle-aged husbands feel they are being neglected. Show you care about his feelings and be enthusiastic about his hobbies.

Bill's face was lit with enthusiasm.

"I know just the place! The Lake District! We can take the train up north, hire bikes and tour round some of our old haunts. Do you remember the youth hostel and that quaint old pub? What was it called — the Shepherd's Rest? Yes, that was it."

"I remember the woods — you picked an armful of bluebells — but they didn't last." Lilian's eyes suddenly misted at the memory but he didn't notice.

"It'll be great to get out of the city for a few days. And I promise, no camping. We'll find an inn where we can stay the night. You'll be able to rest your poor old bones in comfort."

He grinned like a child who had just been promised a special treat.

"Well, if you really think we can do it . . ." Lilian said, still hesitant.

She just didn't feel she would be able to keep up with Bill now. She wasn't the slim young thing, bursting with energy, she had been in those days.

Yet what was the alternative? What would happen if she refused? He seemed so set on the idea he might even take off on his own!

Bill suddenly looked very solemn.

"Wait a minute," he said, his eyes and voice serious. "We can't do it. It's impossible."

"What do you mean impossible? Why is it impossible?"

"Cyclists all wear Lycra shorts these days and I can't see you squeezed into Lycra shorts!" he said, and ducked as she threw a cushion at his head.

THE May afternoon was warm and cloudy when they set off from the cycle hire shop at Windermere. It was the kind of day when it might rain later, but right now was perfect for cycling, with dry roads and just enough heat in the air to be comfortable.

Lilian gave a little scream of alarm as she wobbled dangerously at first, but she quickly found her balance and was surprised at just how easily she fell into the steady pedalling rhythm she thought she had forgotten. Soon they were spinning along together, avoiding the main roads wherever possible.

The views were magnificent, wide expanses of calm water stretched out before them with every turn of the road.

Forced to stop for a breather at the top of a steep hill, they were both awed into silence by the breathtaking sight of the lake, bathed in golden light from the late afternoon sun.

"I had forgotten how beautiful it all is," Lilian said at last. "Perhaps if they could see this, the children might begin to understand why you wanted to come here."

The family had thought they had gone quite mad, of course, but with the peculiar patience of grown-up children who feel they have to humour their ageing parents' behaviour, no matter how eccentric it may appear, they duly waved them off on the train.

"I could sit here for ever," Bill said finally, "but I suppose we'd better start looking for somewhere to spend the night."

Reluctantly, they turned away from the magic of the sunset and remounted the bicycles. Lilian winced as the hard leather of the saddle cut into her thighs, grateful that the next stretch of road was downhill. Her legs felt like lead and it would take every ounce of willpower to force them into action again.

"Do you recognise this road, Lil?" Bill called to her. "Wasn't it around here somewhere that we stayed in the youth hostel? Or was that at Coniston?"

"It was much too long ago for me to remember details like that," she panted. She still hadn't got her breath back after that last hill and was feeling very tired. "It's probably all changed since we were here anyway."

"That looks like a pub up ahead. Maybe we can stop there for the night if they have a room. Are you very tired?"

"Not a bit," Lilian lied, and thought longingly of a long soak in a hot bath with lashings of perfumed salts to ease her aching muscles.

"But we've come quite a distance for the first day and I'd be quite happy to stop here if you want to," she added, praying he wouldn't suggest they could manage another ten miles before nightfall.

"It looks a bit like the Shepherd's Rest as I remember it," said Bill. But as they drew nearer they saw a brightly painted sign hanging over the door.

"No, it can't be. This place is called the Blue Bell Inn. What do you think? Shall we give it a try?"

Ten minutes later Lilian laid her "luggage", a single bulky saddlebag, on the huge double bed which almost filled the tiny attic room at the back of the inn. It was growing dark now but through the open window she could smell the woody fragrance of hundreds of trees reaching out to the mountains in a thick green blanket.

A bath and change of clothes found them both refreshed and surprisingly hungry.

"I'm starved," Bill said, as delightful aromas wafted up from the kitchen.

"Me, too." Lilian nodded. "The fresh air has given us an appetite."

"And the exercise! I told you it would do you good, didn't I?"

The menu was simple but very good. Lilian chose venison in a red wine sauce and enjoyed every mouthful.

Bill's mixed grill was served on an enormous platter and was big enough to satisfy even his appetite, though he still managed to follow it down with a huge chunk of apple pie smothered in cream.

By the time the waitress brought the cheese, Lilian, warm and full of delicious food, was trying desperately to stifle her yawns.

The waitress, an exceptionally pretty girl in a very short skirt, approached the table.

"More coffee?" she inquired. Lilian could see Bill's appreciative eyes on the long, slim legs that seemed to go on for ever, and was suddenly glad of the loose skirt hiding her own plump thighs and knees.

"Not for me, thanks." Bill smiled at the girl and Lilian also declined. She wanted nothing more than to stretch out on the big feather bed upstairs and ease her aching muscles.

She rose stiffly from the table and followed Bill out of the dining-room, but instead of heading for the stairs, he took her elbow and guided her towards the lounge bar where the sound of a strumming guitar could be heard.

Summer Nocturne

PURPLE shadows grow and gather,
  Mists the soaring mountains crown.
Over mantled moor and heather
Shades of night come softly down.

In the west the sun is dying,
Wavelets lisp a lullaby.
Ragged wings of ravens flying
Trace dark patterns on the sky.

Splendour to the night is given
Where, beyond the shadow-bars,
Silver moon, the ship of Heaven,
Sails amid a sea of stars.

Mountains melt in velvet vastness;
In the glen, a waking light
Glows against the growing darkness
Of this spangled summer night.
— *Brenda G. Macrow*

Torridon, Highland.

Gordon Henderson.

"I was talking to the barmaid before you came down," he said, "and she told me they've got a country and western singer on tonight. Let's go and listen for a while, shall we?"

The singer was good and Lilian enjoyed the music, even joining in some of the choruses but, as the evening wore on and her eyelids grew heavier, she longed for the sanctuary of the bedroom. She gave another huge yawn.

"I'm absolutely shattered," she apologised. "Would you mind very much if I slipped off upstairs?"

"Of course not. Off you go," Bill said, his voice kind and full of concern. "You look completely worn out. It's all been a bit much for you, old girl, hasn't it?"

"There's no need to go on as if I'm in my dotage," she was stung into replying. "I'm not used to it, that's all. I'll be fine once I've had a good night's sleep."

"Of course you will. On you go then. I won't be long. I just want a word with some of the locals first."

As she climbed the stairs she saw Bill deep in conversation with the blonde barmaid, her fairness a striking contrast to Bill's raven locks.

For one brief moment Lilian wondered if he might be secretly tinting his hair, but she pushed the thought aside.

Nonsense, she told herself! I'd know if he was doing something like that. Of course I would. Wouldn't I?

LILIAN woke late next morning and found her husband missing and a note pinned to her pillow. *Thought it best to let you rest. Gone exploring. Back before lunch.*

She couldn't believe it. He had gone off without her and for all she knew he could be off exploring with his friendly barmaid from last night.

She ate a late breakfast in solitude, then sat by the window watching the road while her fingers beat out an impatient tattoo on the sill. It was after twelve before she caught sight of Bill's tall figure striding down the hill.

The broad smile he wore as he approached told her he'd been enjoying himself thoroughly — but where and with whom?

"Well, did you have a good time?" Her voice sounded more brittle than she had intended. *Don't make a fuss about unimportant incidents, be patient and supportive at all times,* the article had said.

How she hated that psychologist and her smug advice!

Aloud she asked, "Did you find what you were looking for, then?"

"I certainly did. Come on, there's something I want you to see." He beckoned her to follow him and together they walked back along the road in the direction from which he'd just come.

"This way," he said and shepherded her along a narrow path which disappeared into the trees.

"Where are we going?" she asked, but he raised a cautionary finger to his lips.

"You'll see when we get there," he said.

Fifteen minutes later they rounded a sharp bend between the trees and found themselves in a clearing. All around the trees stood tall and green, with only an occasional rustle of leaves or birdcall breaking the stillness.

A weathered old bench stood in a patch of sunlight, and Lilian had a strange feeling of déjà vu as she smelled the wonderful aroma of pine and moss and woodland flowers.

The air hung sweet and hazy, misted just above the grass where the sun hadn't yet reached. Under the shady arms of the trees, she could see a carpet of bluebells spreading out as far as the eye could see.

"Do you know what I found out last night?" Bill was saying. "The Blue Bell really is the Shepherd's Rest! The present owner changed the name when he bought the place about ten years ago. Can you believe it? It's the very same inn we visited all those years ago.

"I've spent the entire morning looking for this particular spot. We brought a picnic here one afternoon, do you remember?"

Lilian nodded, speechless. Of course she remembered. The memory of that long-ago afternoon was as green as the wooded slopes and as tender as the fragile blue flowers which Bill had claimed were exactly the same colour as her eyes. It was the day he had first told her how much he loved her.

"Look," he was saying now. "You can still see where I carved our initials on this bench. This is why I wanted to come back here, you see. I was hoping we could recapture something of the old days."

The bench was warm against her skin as she silently traced the worn initials with a careful finger. Her blue eyes filled with tears and she couldn't speak for the tight band that held her throat like a vice.

Bill left her side for a few seconds and she saw him pick a single blossom, a slender stem of green topped with a delicate cup of exquisite blue petals.

Holding the flower against her cheekbone he studied the effect.

"A perfect match," he breathed in wonder. "You know, you haven't changed a bit. You're still the same beautiful girl I married."

Lilian swallowed the outsize lump in her throat and managed a tremulous smile.

"That's better," he said, then hesitated for a moment. "I know you'll think this is silly, but I've been worried about you these last few months. Sometimes you looked so sad and distant, as though there was something preying on your mind.

"I even had a word with the doctor, but he said I must simply be patient, and as considerate as possible as you were probably just going through a mid-life crisis."

Her sudden burst of laughter startled him but he soon joined in, plainly delighted to see her so happy again.

As he gathered her into his arms, Lilian mentally tore the magazine, the article and the psychologist's advice to shreds and watched the flimsy fragments vanish forever among the bluebells of love. □

A Dream To Share

by P.D.R. Lindsay

I LOVED my Nan and she loved me. We were comfortable with each other — like a pair of well-broken-in ballet shoes. It was Nan, of course, who taught me to love ballet. And Nan who showed me how to dance.

"You shouldn't listen to your nan," my mum said again and again. "She's a great one for romancing." And she laughed, but then sighed. She didn't see things the way we did.

She never said that Nan was lying, because she didn't want to hurt her feelings. But when a tale grew fancier, she would say, "Mum." And the word would be all drawn out, and sound like a warning.

"Well, it's the way I remember it," Nan would always protest, her voice suddenly quivery and sorrowful. But then her dimples would flick into view, and she'd wink at me.

"Then time and your imagination have done something funny to your memory," my mum would say sternly.

But Nan laughed every time.

"My memory is mine," she'd say. "Both it, and my imagination, are fine."

This time it was a tale about dancing. My mum frowned but Nan chuckled, like bathwater down the plug hole.

"I was just telling one of my ballet stories to Tasha." She managed to sound all hurt and put out as she patted my head softly, one eye swiftly closing at me.

"That's the problem," Mum said.

I couldn't see what the problem was. Nan was telling me about the night she'd danced with Nureyev. I knew all about him — he was one of my heroes, too. I longed to be like Nan and dance with a real ballet company.

"Don't you encourage her," my mum warned Nan. "She's just like you — she hasn't the build for a dancer. A couple of plum puddings you two are!"

I looked at her reproachfully.

"Just 'cos you can twist your dad round your finger," she went on, "and persuade him to pay for lessons." She sighed. "You can't

The People's Friend

make me think that it'll make life any easier for you by wanting to dance." She sighed again and thumped the Christmas pudding mixture around the bowl.

But I was like Nan and loved dancing. We were ever so excited because one of the big professional companies was coming to town to perform the Nutcracker Ballet for Christmas.

Twelve local children would be chosen to dance the parts of the children at the party. One lucky girl would be Clara — the child who is given the magic nutcracker — and have a solo to dance.

All I could think of was the auditions. I ached to be Clara — but I'd happily settle for any of the children's parts.

"No point you going to audition, is there, Dumplin'?" my dad said kindly.

"Why not?" My voice rose.

I breathed in and out quickly and nipped my lips together. Don't snap back, Nan's eyes warned me, or you won't get to go. I held my tongue firmly between my teeth.

"Only Mrs T.'s top students were asked," Mum supplied.

"Well, the audition is open to anyone with a grade two exam merit pass," I said carefully. "Mrs T. didn't say I couldn't go."

Dad looked at Mum, who was moving her mouth about as though she was eating lumpy potatoes. Nan coughed twice in the long pause.

"I'll take her." She looked at both of them. "Ten o'clock, isn't it, Tasha?"

Mum's mouth tried a smile and she stopped stirring the rum into the dried fruit.

"That'll be two children on the loose then," she said severely.

Nan attempted to look hurt, chuckled instead, and pulled a face at her.

"If you can drive us down to the Opera House, Ted —" she said to my dad "— we can do our Christmas shopping afterwards."

Mum opened her mouth, then paused. Finally she said, "Don't do anything silly." I know she meant both of us.

The Opera House was quiet, dim and secretive, not a bit like it looked when you went in the evening to a performance. The main doors were closed and shuttered.

"It'll be open round the back," Nan said, leading me on.

Sure enough, half way down the side alley, a door was propped open. Taped to the dirty glass was a note: *Children's Auditions.*

I took Nan's hand, she squeezed tight, and we went inside.

ALL the ballet mums were there and my teacher, frazzled and harried by their demands. Mrs T. looked at me, then closed her eyes. Nan led me past to join the other children.

There were several ballet teachers and about fifty hopeful students. The clatter and noise we made was swallowed up, muffled by the heavy velvet curtains and that prickly plush seating. It was spooky.

I edged closer to Nan. The curtains bulged and swayed. I reached out

RETURNING from Cortachy in north Angus by way of the carefully restored Castle of Inverquharity — with its rose-red stone, it makes a fine picture from the roadside — I noticed that the wild roses, often called dog-roses, were now in full flower.

June brings the roses!

And very bonnie they looked in their pink, white and yellow. But I began to wonder — why dog-roses?

Dogs care nothing for the scent of flowers, so presumably the dog-rose is so called to distinguish it from the garden rose and the sweet briar.

It's a queer trick of language that some common plants are called after animals.

The violet without a perfume is the dog-violet; the parsnip of the hedgerow is the cow-parsnip; the coarser mushroom is the horse-mushroom.

I mentioned the sweet briar. It has a deliciously aromatic perfume, and a leaf rubbed between the fingers is quite apple-like in scent.

To find another wild rose, called the burnet-rose, you must look, not in the hedgerows, but on windswept moor ground, or on links by the sea.

It grows low on the ground, as if huddling out of the wind, its tiny leaves crowded together, stems bristling with prickles, its white flowers in miraculous profusion.

Poet Hugh McDiarmid called it: "The little white rose of Scotland, that smells sharp and sweet, and breaks the heart."

The White Rose of Scotland.

---

to hold on to her sleeve, just in case.

"All students auditioning please come up on stage," a man's voice said. An arm made a gap between the curtains and pointed to the stage door down in the orchestra pit.

"Will someone please raise this curtain?" the voice continued, sounding like Dad when he's had a long day at work.

We crowded together on the stage. There were four boys amongst us, all very proper in white T-shirts, black tights and black shoes.

"Thank goodness, some boys," the voice said. "You go off stage and sign up with Mrs Taglione." They didn't even have to audition!

I stretched my neck and saw that Mrs T. was standing at the side, waiting for them.

The People's Friend

"Wish I were a boy," I whispered to the girl next to me. She wrinkled her nose and edged away.

Below us, the ballet director was in a huddle with the local ballet teachers, who cast little glances over their shoulders at us. Wisps of their conversation drifted towards me.

I looked for Nan. She was sitting in a row of mothers smiling up at me.

"It isn't fair," I wanted to shout to her. "They're asking the teachers who's best. This isn't an audition!" I opened my mouth and she shook her head at me.

"You lot, move that way." The man was pointing at us as he spoke and sorting us into lines.

"Can't he say please?" I muttered to my neighbour, who shrugged.

Dancers from the company peeped at us from the wings. The teachers peered up from the first row of seats. I felt terrible.

From my place at the back, I watched carefully as we were shown the steps. Easy-peasy, I thought. I always learned steps quickly.

Once we began to dance, it was fun. I ignored the whispers from the wings, the eyes watching from the front. When it came to Clara's dance, I was the first to remember it all.

"Pity you haven't a dancer's body to go with that quick brain," the man said to me. Then he beckoned twelve girls forward and told the rest of us to sit down and be quiet.

"Waste of money paying for lessons for that kid," I hear someone say in the wings beside me. "She's like a pear with feet."

Someone else snickered. I sighed. I'd had that said of me before though I was hardly overweight!

I looked at my feet. They were long and slim, with a dancer's high arches. It was just the rest of me that didn't fit.

I'd just hoped that, this time, they'd have had parts for real children. The Nutcracker story began with a children's Christmas party, after all.

I watched Jenny's skinny long legs stumble through Clara's dance for a second time. I had done it right the first time, but she was chosen to be Clara.

Eight other scrawny girls were picked and we were told to go home. I stomped off to join Nan and Mrs T.

"I'm sorry, Natasha," Mrs T. said to me. "It is so hard for girls who love dancing, but aren't the right build," she added to Nan.

"Ah, but Tasha will always be important to ballet," Nan told her. "Where would any performer be without an audience?"

Mrs T. nodded, smiled at me, and went to tutor the chosen thirteen.

"How do you feel?" Nan asked.

I pulled a face at her. There were no words to tell how the disappointment felt. Even my teeth seemed to hurt.

"I did hope . . ." I began, then shrugged. There was no use complaining.

I knew I was too dumpy to be a ballet dancer. Nan and I were both that shape and . . . I blinked.

Nan had said she had danced with Nureyev. I looked hard at her and opened my mouth. She looked right back.

She had described every detail over and over again. It must be true.

I shut my mouth with a snap as understanding blazed, like fireworks, inside my head. Now I knew what Nan meant about her memory and why Mum always wondered what she'd tell me next.

I started to speak, but Nan winked. She knew.

"Come on," she said. "The others are going, we should move, too."

I caught her hand gratefully and she squeezed it. Then, as we walked past the orchestra pit door, she gave me a push towards it.

"Quick," she said.

I opened the door, slipped through and scampered down the passage to the stage. I crept forward to the front, into the prompt corner and sat down quickly, hiding myself among the folds of the curtain.

NO-ONE came and told me off as I watched the rehearsal. No-one came and asked me to help Jenny learn Clara's part. I was ignored. If this had been in a book, Jenny would break her leg and I would be asked to dance . . . But this was real life. I watched and remembered.

I knew what I would do. That night, I would lie in bed and close my eyes and recall all I'd seen until I could dance Clara's part in my head.

And, every night, until the company left, I would go to bed, shut my eyes, switch on my memories and use my imagination. Then I, not Jenny, would dance Clara in each performance.

I smiled so much my face ached. Easy-peasy!

Clever Nan. That was how she had danced with Nureyev . . .

Still, I did wonder why Mum worried.

"It's not wrong, is it?" I asked, as we pushed through the Christmas crowds.

Nan looked at me.

"To use your imagination like that, I mean?" I said.

She stopped in the middle of the pavement. People muttered and pushed round us.

"You need your hopes and dreams," she said. "Sometimes you can't do the things you want to, but your imagination can." She paused, searching for the right words.

"Your imagination can let you do things the way you dream of doing them. You just have to be careful who you share those dreams with."

"Clever Nan." I put my arm around her and moved her on.

"No point being bitter about what can't be helped." She patted my hand. "We didn't ask to be born with this shape, but we don't have to let that stop us dancing, or doing anything else."

She chuckled again and noticed the café.

"Let's warm up with a hot chocolate and you can tell me what it was like to dance Clara's part." She grinned at me and I grinned back.

"Easy-peasy," I replied. "After all, I learned the dance first!" □

A CUP
Kindne

ELSIE ANDREW wouldn't have known it was her birthday if the usual card hadn't come from America the day before. It stood on the dresser now, a reminder of the passing years. As she tied a scarf over her head, her lined, weatherbeaten face looked back at her from the pitted mirror.

"Eighty-six!" she said aloud, but she couldn't grasp it. It was just numbers. True, her joints ached until she got herself going in the

Klim Forster.

by Robyn Johns

morning, but she felt all right.

Or did she? Since Mrs Richards had come into her life, somehow she wasn't sure.

She stoked the range, then went up the garden to see to the chickens. By the time she got back, the kettle was singing on the hob, and for a while she sat at the window with a mug of tea, watching the October sun lift the mist from the meadow.

Back outside, she raked leaves off the grass, wanting to get through as much as she could before Mrs Richards stopped her.

When she heard the click of the gate, Elsie was up the ladder with her mouth full of nails. It was too late to get down.

"Mrs Andrew!" Mrs Richards hurried forward to grasp the ladder. "Come down this minute. Have you ever thought what would happen if you slipped?"

Elsie hadn't. It didn't do to wonder things like that when you lived alone with half an acre of land to tend.

But she climbed down and mildly accepted the scolding. It was a small price to pay for the company of her new friend.

Elsie liked looking at Mrs Richards. She liked her pretty hair and her soft, city skin. In her scarlet anorak and shiny boots, she was a person from another world. The village had never seen anyone like Mrs Richards.

"Felt wanted tacking down," she said simply.

"Then you should have waited for me. Haven't I promised to come over every day and do what needs to be done?"

Elsie watched Mrs Richards carry the ladder back to the shed and shut the door firmly.

In the kitchen, Mrs Richards produced a bulky parcel from her bag. It was an electric kettle.

"Now you can make tea in the morning without depending on the range."

Elsie thanked her shyly, but in her heart she couldn't see herself using it. She was used to her range. It was a friend of long standing.

Mrs Richards sat Elsie in her chair.

"I've told you before," she said. "You do too much for a woman of your age. You must be sensible and let others help you."

Against her better judgment, Elsie allowed herself to be persuaded. She wanted to please this new friend who was so kind, and, come to think of it, she was a bit tired. I can always get going again later, she thought.

Only, somehow, she couldn't. When Mrs Richards finally left, all the zest and energy with which Elsie had started her day had evaporated.

She had been stopped in full flight and now she felt deflated. She couldn't even rouse herself to knit. She stared into the dying embers of the range, thinking how empty the place seemed without the bright, bustling presence of Mrs Richards.

It had started last September when Elsie had been picking apples. Mrs Richards had appeared at the gate in the lane and started talking.

At first she had been shy of this well-groomed and stylish woman, but

Mrs Richards had been so eager, and genuinely delighted when Elsie let her carry the baskets to the shed, that they were soon sitting at the kitchen table having tea.

"We're from London," Mrs Richards told her. "Reggie, my husband, retired this year and we've taken Yew Tree Cottage for a while to see how we like this part of the world. I think we'll stay. It's so wonderfully remote, isn't it?"

"Aye," Elsie agreed. "It is that."

MRS RICHARDS came every day after that, helping in the house and garden. She had the town dweller's relish for all country matters, especially Elsie's chickens.

Elsie taught her the routine of feeding, watering and shutting up at night. Before long, she was relying on Mrs Richards to do it.

Part of Elsie would rather have gone on doing things for herself, but it was good to have someone about the place every day, and she was enjoying the companionship more and more.

She wondered now if perhaps she had been lonely all this time without knowing it.

So Mrs Richards gradually did more while Elsie sat about and did less.

Elsie still had the occasional flash of guilt and a renewal of independence. Her birthday had been one such — and the day Mrs Richards found Elsie trundling the heavy old mower through the orchard was another.

But it proved to be the last. Elsie was flushed and sweating, and Mrs Richards had taken the mower from her in horror.

"There will be no more of that!" she said firmly. "From now on you leave all the heavy work to me."

And because Elsie wanted to go on enjoying long chats, she had agreed.

These talks were the highlight of her days. Elsie especially enjoyed reliving her life as she told Mrs Richards about the village along ago.

"Although the place hasn't changed much. Of course, folk have cars, there's combines and chemicals and whatnot. And the fields are much bigger. But folk themselves are much the same."

"They must think you're wonderful, the way you've kept all this going by yourself."

"Folk here are used to working hard." Elsie looked at her mildly. "There's nothing wonderful about it. It's either that or go under."

She leaned forward to riddle the range, but Mrs Richards pushed her gently back and did it herself.

"Did your husband come from the village?" she asked.

"We were at the village school together." Elsie smiled at the memory.

"All of us kids crowded into one big room with two teachers, one at each end. It's been closed this many a year — that solicitor has it now, calls it The Old School House.

"George used to pull my hair from behind. I hated him at first, but we got to courting and ended up married for forty-five years."

"Did you have any children?"

"I had a girl, Rebecca. She married an American airman and went to live in South Carolina. Over forty years ago now, that was."

"Don't you ever see her?"

Elsie gazed through the window to the meadow where a horse was munching at the hedge.

"No," she said at last. "We write sometimes and I get cards at Christmas and birthdays.

"She wanted me to go out there when George died but I wouldn't leave here. As long as she's well and happy — that's what matters."

She fell quiet, still watching the horse.

"She's a grandmother herself now. It's funny how you don't notice the years slipping by."

By now Elsie was spending hours in her chair while Mrs Richards took over.

"Now that winter's coming on," Mrs Richards said one day, "I don't think you should trail all the way to the village shop. Just give me your list and I'll do it. I can get your pension, too."

It had been her one independence, but looking at the gathering November gloom, Elsie found it easy to agree.

By December she wasn't leaving the cottage at all. There was no denying it, for the first time in her life Elsie was feeling her age. It looked as if Mrs Richards was right — she had been doing too much.

By the middle of January, she had taken to lying in her old brass bed under the sloping roof until Mrs Richards had let herself in downstairs.

She would listen for the clatter of the range being cleared and coals being shovelled, and after a while Mrs Richards would appear with a tray of tea.

Later, Elsie would dress and come down to sit by the fire. By then Mrs Richards would have cleaned out the cottage and seen to the chickens.

Elsie relied on Mrs Richards now and sometimes she wondered if this was how life would have been if Rebecca had never met her American. Certainly, as the weeks went by, Mrs Richards began to feel like the daughter she had lost.

Tantallon Castle, East Lothian

THREE MILES east of North Berwick, Tantallon Castle stands dramatically on the edge of a sheer cliff overhanging the roaring sea below.

The castle dates from the 14th century and was a stronghold for the powerful Douglas family. It was strengthened to make it impregnable against invaders — the walls are an astonishing 14 feet thick!

TANTALLON CASTLE, EAST LOTHIAN : J CAMPBELL KERR

IN the middle of February, heavy clouds gathered over the meadow and feathers of snow began to fall. Mrs Richards tied a bright silk scarf over her hair.

"I'd better get back," she said. "Reggie isn't very well.

"I've seen to the hens and I'll shut them up on my way out. You'll be all right, won't you?" She was looking at Elsie anxiously.

"I'm going up to bed to keep warm," Elsie said. "I think we're going to have a heavy fall."

Mrs Richards, going down the path, was soon hidden by the falling snow. The wind was rising, and before long the landscape was obscured by a whirling mass of white flakes.

Elsie got into bed and listened to the wind howling in the chimney. It buffeted the windows in a fury, piling snow high on the sills.

It snowed heavily through the night. Next day Elsie stayed upstairs, waiting for the familiar sounds which meant Mrs Richards had arrived.

But the day wore on and she didn't come. There was no fire in the cottage, and soon a damp chill settled in every corner.

Elsie crept along to her bathroom, clutching a blanket round her shoulders. Still thinking Mrs Richards would come, she got back into bed to wait.

All through the day the wind moaned and snow hurled itself against the windows. Fitfully, Elsie slipped in and out of sleep, losing all sense of time and place.

By the second morning the wind had dropped. It was still snowing, but slowly now. Surely Mrs Richards would come today?

Suddenly she remembered the hens. The shock of it hit her like a thunderbolt, and gave her the strength to struggle from her bed.

She pulled a coat over her night things. What had come over her? In all her years she had never done such a thing! To neglect yourself was one thing, to forget the creatures that depended on you was another.

From the window she looked at a white, deserted world. In the icy kitchen, the range stared at her, dead and cold.

From the kitchen window she could see another great drift where once the lawn had been. She knew she was cut off from the rest of the world, and felt suddenly afraid.

But at the thought of her poor, frozen hens, she pushed her feet into damp wellingtons.

The snow creaked under foot and came over the top of her boots, but she made her way up the garden. A germ of her old determination rekindled itself, and she kept going.

As she approached the hen-house a violent and indignant squawking set up inside, and Elsie felt a surge of relief.

It's more than I deserve, she thought grimly. Serve me right if I'd lost them all.

Round the hen-house were the tell-tale marks of hares and rabbits — and the unmistakable imprint of a fox.

A Cup Of Kindness

Elsie fed the birds and managed to break enough ice on the barrel to give them water. She talked to them all the while, forgetting her own predicament in her concern.

Then, carefully stepping in her own footprints, she made her way back to the house. She knew she would have to get warm — and quickly.

Her eyes fell on the electric kettle. She filled it, plugged it in and sat watching it. A few minutes later, as she poured boiling water into the teapot, she felt a flicker of triumph.

The hot tea revived her enough to wonder if she could tackle the range. She took the bucket and went outside again. The snow had drifted heavily against the coalhouse door, and Elsie had to pull with all her remaining strength to get it open. She half filled the bucket and dragged it through the snow to the house.

Soon the kitchen glowed in the firelight. Elsie had drunk some soup, changed into dry clothes, and warmth was seeping through her body.

The snow wasn't frightening any more, it was beautiful. She could remember her mother telling her about winters like this. She had raised a family of nine in conditions far more primitive than these.

Why — at Elsie's age her grandmother had still been working in the fields! That was the stock from which she sprang.

"What's the matter with me?" she wondered aloud. "Why have I given up trying?"

The snow stopped, but Elsie saw no-one. Gradually, she returned to her old self.

She made herself hot food each day, and gained strength hour by hour. She'd forgotten how good it was to be mistress in her own house, and to feel the satisfaction of things done her way.

AFTER a few days, she felt strong enough to take her spade and move some of the snow from the path to the lane. For the first time, the milkman was struggling through the drifts, dragging milk churns and loaves behind him on a sledge. He stopped at her gate and found her flushed and bright-eyed.

"No need to ask how you're getting on, Mrs Andrew!" He grinned. "You look as though you're enjoying yourself."

"I am." She smiled back at him. She fetched a jug, and he dipped a ladle into the churn and filled it for her.

"This is like the old days, so they tell me," he said. "If it goes on like this we shall have to have an airlift!" He shook his head ruefully.

"At least you're better off than some. Have you heard about the Richards?

"Mr Richards come down with pneumonia just before the snow, and they got it worse than anyone. Power lines down over that end. No electric and no phone — no-one can reach them yet, drifting's that bad."

The thaw came a week later. Elsie heard nothing from Mrs Richards, but from the milkman she heard they were all right.

It was in the first week in March, when she was chopping wood for the range, that she heard the click of the gate.

Looking up, she saw Mrs Richards coming towards her through the trees.

Mrs Richards looked at the neat pile of wood and the line of washing blowing in the wind.

Inside the cottage, she saw everything neat and shining, with the old iron kettle singing gently on the hob. The shiny electric kettle was back in its box on the dresser. For the moment its day was over.

"You've heard about Reggie?" Mrs Richards said. "This is the first time I've been able to leave him. These have been the most terrible weeks of my life! I've been worried sick about him — and you. Until I heard you were coping."

Elsie put the teapot on the table.

"It's a case of having to," she said. "When you're on your own, if you don't do a thing yourself it stays undone. For a while there, I forgot that."

Mrs Richards looked at the old lady. Her hair was pulled into a tidy knot and her apron was fresh and clean.

"You mean you'd forgotten — because of me?"

"I shouldn't have let you do so much for me," Elsie said simply. "I liked you coming here, that's why I didn't say anything, but it doesn't do to lean too much on other folk until you have to. Plenty of time for it then."

Mrs Richards nodded, staring thoughtfully into her cup.

"I've really come to say goodbye," she said at last.

Elsie looked at her without surprise.

"Oh, yes?"

"The summers here are lovely, of course, but Reggie could never stand another winter like that. To tell you the truth, neither could I.

"We're going back to London on Friday to stay with my sister while we hunt for a flat."

Elsie nodded.

"It can be harsh up here," she agreed. "I expect it takes a bit of getting used to. A lot of folk come up this way thinking they'll settle, but not many do. You need to be born to it."

A little later, Elsie pulled on her coat and walked Mrs Richards to the gate. There was a hint of the end of winter, and in several places bulbs were showing through.

"Will you be all right when we've gone?"

"I'll be all right as long as I keep going." Elsie looked at her steadily. "I've learned something this winter. The less you do — the less you want to do."

Mrs Richards leaned forward and kissed her cheek.

"I've learned something, too," she said. "They say you can kill with kindness, don't they?"

Elsie remembered the day she nearly gave up.

IN early July one can hardly step out of doors without bumping into a family in feathers.

It may well be a family of starlings — the offspring screeching for food, the parents stuffing them as fast as they can.

In the woods it may be robins. The young birds are speckled in brown, and can hardly be called "red-breasts" at this stage.

Some young birds, like thrushes, are very quiet as nestlings and even as fledglings. On arriving with food, the adult birds are only greeted with silent, gaping mouths.

This is very different from the noisy behaviour of young rooks and starlings. But then they are in safe places — in holes and in the tree tops — well out of harm's way. The ability to remain silent and motionless may serve other young birds in good stead when a stoat or a cat comes prowling nearby.

Walking among the fields and hedgerows, you may well disturb a family of partridges at this time of year. The parent birds will scurry in mad semi-circles, wings drooping, voices raised in a frenzy of clattering.

When this happens, you must keep perfectly still. If you search in the grass you may find one chick here, another there, but it's better to step gingerly and pass on, leaving the family to re-unite.

The fledgling thrushes in my drawing had taken a viewpoint from which they could watch the ways of the world around them. But they were making no comment meantime.

Young thrushes.

"Aye," she agreed. "I've heard it said."

She turned back into her garden. There were still two hours of daylight left, enough to start breaking up the ground for the early potatoes.

As she eased the spade into the earth, a blackbird struck up his song from a nearby branch and a robin hopped about her feet with a bright, expectant eye.

Elsie heard the wind rushing through the bare branches above her head, and the waters tumbling along the brook.

The sounds refuelled her, somehow. She felt part of them and was happy. Happy enough to hum as she dug. □

The Saddle,
Glen Sheil.

Fair Kintail

IN fair Kintail, the iris bright
  With golden spears salutes the dawn
And apple trees in pink and white
Shed scented blossoms on the lawn,
While rowans, trees of fairy lore,
Stand guard by many a cottage door.

The ancient hills, in beauty bare,
Are clustered under opal skies.
The Sisters cloudy chaplets wear,
And sunlight on Loch Duich lies,
While o'er The Saddle grey gulls
    wheel
Above the cleft of green Glen Shiel.

And when the golden sun has set
Behind the jagged peaks of Skye,
And Castle Donan's silhouette
Upon its island charms the eye,
Such beauty with me ever stays
To lure me down remembered ways.
                    — *Brenda G. Macrow.*

by Valerie Edwards

94

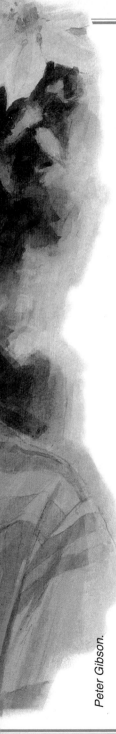

Peter Gibson.

The Artist's Model

MARIE had been just a young child when she'd decided she wanted to be an artist's model. To be the centre of someone's complete attention — someone's masterpiece — would be wonderful!

She fidgeted a little on the straight-backed chair as she thought back to the day she'd set herself this ambition.

She'd been six, well nearly seven — the day out had been a birthday treat. Her mother's brother, Uncle Frank, had arrived unexpectedly and swept both herself and her mother off for the day.

She remembered lunch at the fancy café — egg and beans and chips, and the never-to-be-forgotten Knickerbocker Glory. And then the sudden torrential downpour as they'd wandered round the shops.

They'd rushed headlong to find shelter, but all the doorways were full. So they'd ended up in the one place they'd never have dreamt of visiting — an art gallery.

It must have been an amateur exhibition, she thought now. The elderly man snoozing at the desk hadn't even looked up as they came, dripping and squelching, up the stairs.

Mum and Uncle Frank had simply wandered over to

the window, staring out at the rain, whilst warming their hands on the radiator. But she had walked up and down the rows of pictures, standing on tiptoe to study every one.

Mostly, they seemed to be of bowls of fruit — apples, oranges, bananas — or trees and streams and blue skies, with lots of white frilly clouds. But, right in the very middle, there were pictures of people.

They were so beautiful, the ladies in those paintings. Some were pictured standing with their hands joined together, some sitting, with their knees crossed. There were smiling faces, serious faces, long dresses, short skirts . . . Some held flowers and one was reading a book.

She'd been entranced. Where did these people come from?

"You have to pose," her mother had said, dismissively. "Now stop asking questions and come away. The rain's stopped. Uncle Frank wants to get on."

Uncle Frank grinned, saying he was ready for a cup of tea.

Marie had never forgotten that trip to the gallery. To have your portrait painted, and displayed, for everyone to see and admire, just seemed so glamorous.

WHEN people asked what she was going to be when she left school, she always told them an artist's model. They all laughed, of course — especially the teachers.

Miss Benson, who taught drama and never picked Marie for a part, no matter how many were in the cast, said she simply hadn't a ghost of a chance. And old Mrs Chrysler, who came in specially twice a week to take them for needlework, put her arm round Marie's shoulders and told her it was golden-haired girls like Marilyn Monroe, or royal princesses, that artists wanted to paint.

Marie had looked in her dressing-table mirror, staring at her straight, bobbed hair and unflattering glasses. Perhaps they were all right. She was rather plain. Who'd want a portrait of her?

In the fullness of time, she'd left school, without a backward glance, and went to college to learn office skills. It had all been her mother's idea, and really she couldn't think of a reason for not going along with it.

She'd proved to be quite a good typist — fast and accurate. Then she'd got a job in an estate agent's office.

She smiled to herself now, remembering.

There hadn't been much call for artists' models in Bury.

Once, daringly, she'd applied to the local tech when they'd advertised for a sitter, but she'd been turned down.

They'd had quite a lot of applicants — she'd seen them in the waiting-room when she'd gone for her interview. Golden-haired girls who, if they didn't exactly look like Marilyn Monroe or royal princesses, certainly looked more glamorous than Marie. In the end though they'd chosen a man.

It had been at the tech that she'd met Alan. He was lost — and had asked her if she knew the way to the engineering class. She hadn't known, of course, but somehow or other they'd ended up having a cup of coffee in the café. A year later, they'd married.

MARIE eased herself on the chair. She was starting to feel stiff and she knew, when she stood up, her skirt was going to be badly creased. Surreptitiously, she tried to pull the hem further down. She didn't think he noticed.

The one thing she'd never thought of was cramp. It hit her suddenly, excruciatingly, in her left big toe, running under her instep towards her ankle. Cautiously, she moved her foot forward. Her shoe creaked.

He looked up then, frowned, lips pursed.

"Sorry," she apologised.

As the cramp eased into pins and needles, she studied him covertly. Such a handsome face he had — those dark, intense eyes, that black hair.

I've waited all these years, she thought, amused. Then she giggled. After a second, he joined in.

Then, with a flourish, he held out the sheet of paper he'd been working on.

"Finished," he said in triumph.

She stared down at the round, crayoned face, the smudged blue eyes, the garish red mouth, the thatch of grey hair.

"It's lovely, David," she said, kissing the top of her small grandson's head.

"It's exactly like me. I'm going to pin it up on the wall. Then everyone can see and admire it." She smiled.

It had taken over fifty years, but at last she had fulfilled her dream. Today she had become an artist's model! □

Those Little Things

A little ray of sunshine
On a gloomy winter's day,
A letter from a loved one
Who is many miles away.

A visit from a neighbour
With a little word of cheer,
An unexpected phone call
From a person I hold dear.

A little act of kindness
From a stranger in the street,
A little smile of welcome
From the folk I chance to meet.

A little word of comfort
When my worries get me down,
A funny little incident
That wipes away a frown.

The sound of little children
As they go about their play,
The feeling of contentment
At the closing of the day.

The little smile of wonder
From a baby in its cot.
Just add these all together
And they come to quite a lot...
— Alice Drury.

A Country Girl At Heart

HOLLY'S mother isn't expecting us till late afternoon," Martin said, as they arrived at the Cornish seaside town much earlier than anticipated.

"If we go straight there, she'll start fussing. I don't want her to feel she has to make a meal for us. Why don't we stop somewhere and have a bite just now? I could do with a drink, too. I'm parched!"

"OK by me," Chris agreed.

Martin drove into the carpark next to an attractive pub and soon they were sitting in a shady beer garden with their drinks.

"It's nice here, isn't it?" Chris was taking everything in.

"Yes, it's a good view of the harbour. There's a beach, too — not the best one for surfing. That's over the other side."

Martin, a keen surfer, had been here before.

A girl in a green dress and crisp white apron came up to the table.

"I'll just remove this lot." She expertly stacked plates and glasses left by the previous customers. "Your lunch will be ready in a minute."

"Thanks," Chris said as she turned to go.

by
**Renée
Langdon**

Troels Marstrand.

She looked back at him and their eyes met and held for a second before she moved away.

"Good grief!" Martin exclaimed, catching sight of his friend's expression. "You look as if you've been pole-axed."

"I think I've fallen in love at first sight," Chris finally managed, sounding bemused.

Martin couldn't help laughing.

"You must be on the rebound. It's only two weeks since you split up with Tanya."

"No — I told you — when Tanya said she couldn't face going to Greece with me, it was a relief. It was over between us long ago." Chris shrugged.

99

The People's Friend Annual

"Anyway, how could I say no when Holly's mum offered to put me up? Two weeks in Cornwall with my best friend and his girlfriend might not be everyone's idea of a great break, but, if you don't mind me playing gooseberry, I'm sure it'll be fun." He smiled at Martin and then looked up as the waitress approached.

"Remember you said I was bound to meet some gorgeous girl on the beach, or in the pub, or . . ."

"Yes?"

"I think I've met her," he whispered.

The girl, her light brown hair shining in the sun, put two full plates before them.

"I hope you enjoy your meal."

Her voice had a soft Cornish burr and her mouth curved in a smile.

Chris wanted to drown in her beautiful green eyes; as green as the sea washing the distant sands . . . He ate his lunch in a daydream.

By the time they had finished their leisurely meal, most of the other tables were empty. Chris had been watching the girl clearing tables, talking and laughing with the retreating customers.

Soon the garden quietened and the hum of insects replaced that of human conversation. It was hot and humid and there was only a whisper of a breeze stirring the leaves on the trees.

"I'll leave you to settle up." Martin handed him some money and got to his feet. "I'll wait for you by the car. Give you a chance to have a word with — well, maybe you can make a date." He winked.

He took the car keys from his jeans' pocket and strolled off, jangling them.

The girl came towards Chris with the bill.

Once he'd paid, he stood uncertainly for a moment. Her warm smile gave him courage.

"Would you come out with me?" he blurted out. "Do you think we could meet — go for a drink, or something?"

A ripple of laughter was the response.

"You Londoners don't waste much time, do you?"

"I'm only here for two weeks. I can't afford to waste time," he told her, smiling into her cheerful face.

She looked at him speculatively for a moment and then nodded.

"Why not? I could meet you tomorrow for a picnic, if you like . . . I'm sorry, you didn't tell me your name."

"Chris — Christopher Dymond."

"I'm Tansy," she said. "Tansy Small."

They arranged their meeting, then Chris reluctantly rejoined Martin.

*　　*　　*　　*

Tansy watched him go. The tall young man, with the thick wavy hair, had made quite an impression on her.

"Come on, Tansy. We've got work to do, you know. The washing-up

100

awaits." Her sister, Daisy, came up behind her.

"He looked nice. Passing through or staying?"

"Staying, I guess."

"Hey — you fancied him, didn't you?"

"He asked me out."

"Well, he didn't waste any time!"

"That's what I said." Tansy laughed, and they walked back through the garden and into the kitchen.

As she tidied up in the kitchen, she felt glad that she'd happened to be waitressing that day. She was home for a holiday from the retirement home near Truro where she was a nurse, but had been happy to fill in at the pub for a couple of days. Her parents owned and ran The Blue Anchor with the help of Tansy's three sisters.

Jackie would be back at work tomorrow and Tansy would be free to enjoy the rest of her holidays.

BY 10.30 the following morning, it was already hot and the beach was filling up with holidaymakers. Tansy walked across to the rocks, her bare feet feeling deliciously cool on the wet sand.

Chris was sitting on a flat rock, casually dressed in shorts and a T-shirt. He stood up and waved as soon as he saw her and she waved back, suddenly thinking how attractive he was.

She had brought a picnic lunch and, after swimming and walking together, they ate and talked some more.

The day passed by so quickly, they were taken by surprise when it started to get dark. It seemed natural to walk hand-in-hand as he took her home, and, after arranging to meet again, to kiss on parting.

Lying on the grass on the cliff top the following day, Chris gazed up at Tansy.

"Martin proposed to his girlfriend, Holly, last night," he told her. "They're throwing an engagement party next week."

"Has he known her long?"

"He met her here two years ago when he came down on holiday. He was with some other guys to do some surfing. He drives down quite often and she comes up to London to see him. Now he thinks it's time he settled down and raised a family."

Tansy knew what good friends Chris and Martin were. They'd once shared a flat when Chris had first started work in London. Even after Chris moved into a flat of his own, they'd remained friends.

"You'll come to the party with me, won't you?"

She nodded, and he reached up for her.

"There must be something in the air here."

He rested his palm on her cheek and she kissed him lightly on the lips.

"Come on," she said, getting to her feet. "Remember I'm taking you to Lanhydrock today."

The National Trust property was one of the places she wanted to show

A Gift She Always

TODAY we visited our local garden centre and I came across a plant which brought back memories. It was a small indoor palm.

I found Anne and took her to look at this wee palm plant.

"I'll buy you that, Anne."

"It's a nice thought, dear, thank you, but just leave it there."

Later, as we were sitting by the fire, Anne reminded me of the story about the potted palm.

Anne, before she married me, was a Sunday School teacher.

Every year, they had their annual Sunday School trip. It was usually to Elie or Lower Largo, but one year they decided to go further afield to the town of Leven, seven miles away.

The reason for this change of venue was that they decided to ask Mums to come, too. They could go shopping in Leven if they wished. The mothers had to pay five shillings to help with the cost of the bus.

HARRY, one of Anne's pupils, was aged ten when his father was killed on the laird's estate. Harry's mother was left a widow at the young age of thirty-six.

The laird allowed her to live in the cottage rent-free but it was a struggle for her on a widow's pension. Yet, she was determined that her Harry would be turned out smartly.

She didn't join the other mothers on the Sunday School trip to Leven.

Harry explained to Anne that his mother "had a cold."

Anne knew why she hadn't come — five shillings was money she couldn't afford.

Give her her due, she gave Harry a shilling and three pennies, so that if any of the other children went to buy sweets or an ice-cream, Harry could do the same.

After an enjoyable day on the beach, they all assembled for the bus home.

Anne noticed Harry was clutching a small palm plant.

"Who's that for, Harry?"

"Mother, Miss. She couldn't come on the trip."

Anne says she

him. Tansy loved her home ground passionately and wanted Chris to enjoy the rocky coast and diverse countryside as she did.

AT the engagement party the following week, Tansy was keen to get to know Martin's friends and soon found a chance to speak to Holly.

"Are you going to live in London once you're married then?" she asked.

"Yes." Holly nodded happily. "Martin says it'll be easy for me to get a job there."

"What do you do?"

reasured

was so touched by his kind thought, she had to turn her head away, in case he saw her tears.

Anne was married a few years later and moved to our farmhouse on the Riggin. She lost touch with Harry and his mum, but knew he left the village school and obtained a job in a gents' clothiers in Leven. A few years later, he obtained a post in Manchester.

Harry's mother died at the age of sixty-two and her funeral was at Crail, where she had been born.

Harry was there, dressed in his Sunday best, and Anne spoke to him at the light meal he laid on in a local hotel. She asked if he was married.

No wife, he said, would want him as he was a commercial traveller, away from home from Monday to Friday.

"Did your mother still have your palm plant?" Anne asked.

"Yes, and it's now five feet tall."

"Are you taking it home?"

The Farmer And His Wife

by
John
Taylor

Harry shook his head sadly.

"No, my landlady is not a plant lover. She'd not be too pleased if I went back with it. Yet I can't throw it out. . ."

"Harry, I'd love to keep it for you," Anne said. And she did.

It came to the Riggin and we had it for eleven years until, for some reason, it decided it was time to die and it did, despite the care it was given.

And that was why, when I saw that palm plant in the garden centre, I wanted to buy it for Anne.

"Legal secretary — but not one of those Dickensian ones, you know. We're computerised now!" She laughed.

"Will you like living in London?"

"Sure. Why not? It'll be a change from here. Well, it's not bad in the summer, but it's dead in winter. You must admit that!"

Tansy couldn't understand Holly's feelings. She loved Cornwall all the year round — in the wind and in the rain, when the waves thundered against the rocks and sent up huge fountains of spray, when all the trees leaned inland, bent by the force of the winds off the sea.

The thought of living in London horrified her. Yet that was where Chris lived . . . And she was falling in love with him.

103

They'd had a marvellous two weeks together and the weather had been kind to them. She felt comfortable with him and, when he kissed her, she felt her heart soar.

But could she go to London to be near him? Tansy knew London very well. She had done her training there. Yet her happiest memory was of the day she'd qualified and knew she could at last leave the city.

She didn't think she could bear to live there . . .

Holly moved off to chat to a friend and Tansy saw Chris threading his way through the crowd towards her.

"Where've you been? I've been looking for you." He smiled and suddenly she felt tears at the back of her eyes. He was so dear. How could she bear to lose him?

They said goodbye on the little bridge over the stream at the end of Honeysuckle Lane. The car was loaded up and ready to go, Martin sitting behind the wheel.

"I don't want to leave you. I'll never forget the past two weeks. I love you, Tansy. You know that, don't you?"

Chris's finger touched her cheek and travelled down to her lips.

"I love you, too." She raised her mouth to his.

They clung together, neither wanting to let go.

A toot on the horn disturbed them.

"I have to go."

He kissed her again and tore himself away, running up the lane. He turned once and waved.

"See you at the wedding," he shouted, and was gone.

Tansy flung herself back into her job, glad to have something to concentrate on.

"It's only a holiday romance, my dear," her mother said. "You've just known him a few days. Don't go upsetting yourself if you don't hear from him again."

"He's special, Mum. He really is. Chris won't forget me."

To her delight, Chris rang regularly and visited when he could. They grew even closer, yet never spoke of the future.

It was after Holly and Martin's wedding that things came to a head.

Tansy drove Chris to the station to catch his train back to London and was surprised when he hardly spoke on the journey. Finally, when she pulled in, he turned to face her.

"I can't go on saying goodbye to you!" he cried.

"Coming for weekends and holidays — it's not enough. I know we haven't known each other long, but I want to marry you, Tansy. I love you very much."

When she turned to meet his eyes, he kissed her — a long, deep kiss that sent her pulse racing.

"Please, darling. Say you'll marry me — soon. My flat's big enough for two, and, if you don't like it, we'll —"

"I love you, too, Chris. You know I do, but . . ." She couldn't hide her fears. "You want me to give up my job and move to London." She took a deep breath. "I don't know if I can do that."

"You could get a job in London, at one of the big old folk's homes. It'd be better than the one you've got now — better paid. There's so much to do there. You'd get to like it."

Chris's face was so eager, she felt as though her heart would break. Then she remembered the panic attacks she'd had on the Underground and the feeling that all the buildings and the people would fall and smother her. She'd hated the crowds, the noise, and had been so homesick.

"You know I hate London," she said slowly. "I'm a country girl. I'd feel hedged in. No sea, no moors, no . . . I couldn't bear it, Chris. Couldn't you come and live here?"

"Oh, Tansy." Disappointment make his voice harsh. "How could I get a job here? I'm a civil servant. I've got a job — a good job. You couldn't expect me to give it up."

"You expect me to give up mine."

"It's not the same, and you know it. My job is secure, which counts for a lot these days.

"If you really love me, you'll come to London. It'll be dead down here, now the season's over. There's plenty to do and see in —"

"Don't say it! I don't want to hear it again. Just go, go on." Her voice was unsteady now. "You'll miss your train."

Taking his bag off the back seat, he got out, slamming the door behind him.

Tansy sat with tears streaming down her face.

She'd known it would come to this. Fool, fool, she thought, you've thrown it all away . . .

W HAT'S happened to you? You've had the miseries all week and no mistake."

Old Miss Russell might be ninety-six, wobbly on her pins and frail, but she was very astute.

"Fallen out with that young man of yours, I dare say. The one you met on holiday."

She chuckled as Tansy handed her two pills and a glass of water.

"Never you mind about that, Nosey Parker. Just take your pills."

Miss Russell grinned. She was very fond of her young nurse.

"I bet you five pounds he'll ring this weekend."

"Can you afford it?" Tansy asked, plumping up the pillows. "Won the Lottery, have you?"

But Miss Russell was right.

"I'm sorry," Chris said, when she answered the telephone. "I've been miserable all week. I thought maybe you wouldn't want to hear from me again."

"Of course I do." She almost wept with relief. "I'm sorry, too. It was all my fault. I was horrible, and I've been miserable, too."

"We mustn't quarrel."

"No, we mustn't. It's stupid."

"I love you, darling. I just get so fed up with you being so far away."

"Me, too. I miss you terribly."

"I'm going to put in for a transfer."

Her heart leapt at his words.

"I'll let you know if anything comes up. There must be something outside London.

"It's just that it's likely to take some time. Will you be patient, darling? I'll ring you every week and I'll try to come down again soon. It's not so far really — could be a lot worse."

"Oh, yes — please try."

"Maybe in a couple of weeks. I'll ring and confirm next weekend."

"It'll give me something to look forward to — and I'll try to be patient. I do love you, Chris."

As the weeks passed, they exchanged telephone calls and letters and were able to spend time together at Christmas. Chris applied for several posts but, by the end of spring, was no nearer Tansy.

YOU'RE like a dying duck in a thunderstorm," Miss Russell snapped one afternoon when Tansy was moping around. "What we want's a bit of cheer, not a wet weekend. He's doing his best, you know. Pull yourself together, girl."

The old lady had dozed off in her chair in the sun and had woken with a start, feeling bad tempered. She immediately felt sorry for her words as Tansy's eyes filled with tears.

"Sit down — come on. I'm sorry. I didn't mean to be so sharp. I want to talk to you."

Tansy sat down tentatively.

"You're going about this the wrong way, you know. It's a question of priorities. Which is it to be? Life with him in London, or life without him here? It's a clear choice, and only you can make it."

She paused, looking at Tansy's stricken face.

"Now, you know you can't expect him to come here. He's got a reasonably secure, pensionable job, and certainly can't be expected to give it up — especially if he's thinking of getting married. But if you go up there — to him — you'll be together while he goes on trying for his transfer. He'll get it in the end, you'll see.

"What's the point of wasting time apart? I know the thought of living in the city frightens you, but he'll be there — you'll be together."

Tansy nodded slowly.

"Yes . . . You're right. Suitable vacancies don't come up often. It could be ages — and I really do want to be with him. I've been very selfish . . ."

"We all are, my dear. I'll miss you, but it'll be worth it, you'll see."

The old lady leant forward and patted her knee.

"Think of the money you'll save on telephone calls and stamps," she added with a grin.

That evening, Tansy rang Chris. He sounded a bit low.

"Are you all right?" she asked. "Are you coming down with a cold?"

"No — I'm fine. What about you?"

"Would it be OK if I came up next weekend?" she asked. "I really want to see you." It was the first time she'd volunteered to go to London.

"Great — that'd be marvellous!" He sounded thrilled.

He met her train at Paddington and they fell into each other's arms. As he covered her face with kisses, Tansy knew she'd made the right decision.

"I've given in my notice," she said as soon as she could speak. "I'm coming to London. I want to be with you. I've been a selfish pig and I —"

"You've what?" he cried, holding her at arm's length and looking at her flushed face.

"I've promised to stay on until the end of next month," she told him. "They'll have to advertise, but I expect they'll soon find someone else."

Chris started laughing and Tansy stared at him. Yet she couldn't help smiling.

"You're wonderful — my wonderful, wonderful, Tansy."

"Well, I'm glad you're happy. But I don't —"

"This morning," he interrupted her, "I heard I've got a job in Truro."

Her eyes opened wide.

"Truro?"

"I didn't tell you because I didn't want to raise your hopes. I couldn't believe it when I heard the job was mine. I still find it difficult to take in.

"I was going to tell you — but you pipped me at the post, so to speak. You may have noticed, I was grinning like a Cheshire cat."

"I thought that was because of me." Tansy laughed and they hugged each other joyfully. I don't deserve this, she thought.

"Now," he said, as he picked up her holdall, "when shall we get married?"

"Very soon." She took his hand. "And there's someone special who's going to enjoy every minute of it." □

Storm At Dusk

OMINOUS storm on the distant hill,
Sullen clouds edge closer still,
Flashes of fire light the sky —
Yet still the silvered seagulls fly.

The storm brings gloom to dusking day,
To wispy cirrus, pink and grey;
Soon the skies are overcast,
Menacing, awesome, sinister, vast.

Dusk engulfed by thunderclouds,
Their darkly purple veil enshrouds,
Until a dazzling streak of white
Transforms the scene to eerie light.

Then the crack of fearsome sound,
While echoes through the sky rebound;
Sudden cloudburst, fragrant rain,
This is the thunderstorm's domain.
— Enid Pearson.

FOR some reason, Emily had been contemplating her life with Jim lately.

She blamed it on Christmas, which never failed to make her nostalgic.

Jim was a wonderful man and an excellent father. She knew her life was wonderful by any standards, but she couldn't help craving some romance, a little mystery, some magic. Life had become just a bit too predictable.

She sighed and focused on the beautiful fir tree and the small boy admiring it.

Emily thought it was one of the most heartwarming sights she had ever seen — the Christmas tree lights reflected in the eyes of her grandson, Jordan. At five, he was the perfect age for sharing the pleasures of tree decorating.

"When Grandpa gets back from the shops, he'll be surprised at how much we've done." Carefully, he hung a lumpy dough snowman on the nearest branch.

Emily smiled at the ornament. She could picture her son, Tom, labouring over it. For Emily, as always, seeing the ornaments triggered an avalanche of memories.

"Did you know your daddy made that ornament?"

"My daddy?" Jordan looked stunned at the notion.

"Yes. Now, let's see what we've got wrapped up in this." Emily slit the tape on yet another box.

"Oh," she breathed. "Our angel. Isn't she beautiful? Shall we let Grandpa put this on top of the tree?"

Something

Very carefully, she set down the angel on the mantlepiece. She was truly gorgeous, with clear creamy features and gleaming ebony hair.

I remember that Christmas, Emily thought. Our crops had failed, and we had no money. I was just going through the motions of Christmas for the sake of the kids — until Jim gave me this angel.

Jim had sold his dearest possession, his grandfather's pocket watch, to buy it. When she'd protested, he'd cupped her chin in his hand.

"A black-haired angel for my black-haired angel! Please don't deny me the pleasure!"

Her eyes stung at the cherished memory. Wasn't it proof that they had once had romance in abundance? It was just too bad that there were no more surprises in their relationship, now.

"Look, Grandma, icicles!"

"Those are the same icicles your grandpa had on his tree when he was your age. Do you remember them from last year? They glow after the lights are turned out."

But Jordan was already unwrapping another tissue-wrapped bundle, so Emily started hanging the iridescent icicles.

She felt rushes of pleasure as Jordan held up ornament after ornament. Some were plastic, which she'd found at garage sales; others were antiques she'd inherited from Jim's Aunt Dorothy.

Then there were the ones made

Special

by
Terry Miller
Shannon

Mike Heslop.

by Tom and Susie. You could see the stages of development the children had gone through in the sophistication of the decorations. From crayoned Santas, cut out of cardboard, to various creatures made out of dough and, finally, foam balls covered with bright scraps of fabric . . .

"Wow! What's this?" Jordan had pulled out a bundle and had peeled the paper off.

Emily stifled a smile at the appalled look on his face. In his hand was a plastic head, brilliantly pink and unbelievably ugly.

What was it supposed to be? The moon? A monster? All she knew was that, for some reason, it had special significance for Jim.

She couldn't quite remember why — was it a childhood memento? Something given to him by a loved one? Or something he had won?

She smiled, remembering the way he'd repeatedly repositioned the ornament. He always wanted to maximise its visibility, so no-one would miss it.

"That's something very special to Grandpa," she answered carefully.

"Why?"

"You'll have to ask him about it, sweetheart." She smiled. "Let's take a cocoa break, shall we?"

THEY were in the kitchen sharing a plate of chocolate-chip cookies and sipping their hot drinks when Jim hurried through the back door.

"Whew," he said, shedding his dripping raincoat. "It's pouring! How are you two doing with the tree?"

"You need to put the angel up on top!" Jordan ran to his grandfather and hugged him around his legs.

"Oh, yes, the beautiful black-haired angel." Jim smiled at Emily over his head.

"Want some cocoa?" Emily smiled back at him. "I'll make some whilst you're putting up the angel."

"OK, love." Jim and Jordan headed into the living-room.

Emily could hear them discussing the placing of the angel as she poured milk into the saucepan.

"Grandpa, what's this head?" she heard Jordan asking.

"Oh, that's something special your grandma treasures. I think she had it when she was growing up."

"What?" Emily turned the cooker off and marched into the living-room. "What do you mean? You know it's yours!"

Jim looked at her blankly. "No, it's not."

"But, the way you arrange it and rearrange it, so it'll be in the best position, so everyone will see it . . ."

"Oh, I only do that because I know how much it means to you. I see how carefully you wrap it in tissue paper each year."

"Only because I thought you loved it!"

They burst into laughter. They laughed and laughed, Jordan joining in.

"Who knows where it came from!" Emily gasped.

Colin Gibson's Almanac
August

Young Highland cattle.

AN artist friend of mine, Tim Havers by name, specialises in painting river scenes and famous salmon pools on such rivers as the Tay and the Spey.

He was telling me of an experience he had one August day. He was working in oils on a fairly big canvas on a slope above a fine stretch of river valley.

He said that, in the middle of the day, he decided to go downhill and see if he could get "a spot of lunch" somewhere. His painting was unfinished and the paint was wet, so he left it in the shadow and shelter of a hedge.

When he returned, some time later, he was rather taken aback when he found a bevy of young Highland cattle alongside the hedge.

And he got a shock when he found his canvas with all the paint licked off! So much for his river scene and his morning's work.

I had an equally vexing experience when I was asked to do a painting at Noranmouth on the South Esk.

"Do it when the autumn tints are on the trees," I was told. "That's when it looks at its best."

This is a two-day job, I thought to myself. Everything went well on the first day. The trees and their reflections in the water were beautiful.

But next morning when I arrived, all was different. There had been a bit of rough weather, and the trees were bare. The autumn tints had gone with the wind!

"I always thought it was so ugly!" Jim said.

"Truly hideous!" Emily agreed.

Jim lifted the ornament in his big hands. The face seemed to grin at them.

"Well," he said, slowly. "I guess we can throw it away now."

Emily thought of the years she had taken care of the ornament, wanting to make Jim happy.

He, in turn, had cherished and cosseted it as a token of his love for her, year after year. The ornament itself was nothing. But, as a symbol of their love, it was . . . everything.

"No." Her eyes met his. "Hang it in the very best spot. The way you always have."

And he did. □

Mark Roberts.

by Helen Lincoln

I JUST don't believe it!"

Malcolm Dunbar stared aghast at the fax machine as it coughed out his letter, thoroughly chewed. Gritting his teeth, he fumbled to tug it out and ripped it. Then the machine gave a piercing shriek that did nothing for his headache.

"Sandra!" he yelled above the noise. "Help!"

His young partner popped her head round the door, smiling.

"Malcolm, what are you up to?"

She tapped a button and the shrieking stopped.

"What is wrong with that evil machine?" Malcolm demanded in exasperation.

"It's not evil — it's temperamental like the rest of us." Sandra winked. "It misses Janet Laurie."

Don't we all, Malcolm thought, with an inward sigh.

"Did you make a copy? Good. Here, I'll do it," Sandra offered.

"Oh, yes," Malcolm muttered grumpily. "At least the photocopier was in a good mood this morning. Maybe we should invest in some new equipment, Sandra."

FOR OLD TIMES' SAKE

Sandra chuckled as the letter slipped smoothly through the humming machine.

"Nothing wrong with what we've got. What you need is a new secretary — and you know it."

"I can't get anyone as good as Janet," Malcolm retorted. "That

113

last lot we interviewed were useless."

"Three of them were perfectly adequate. You're too fussy. Janet Laurie spoiled you." Sandra glanced around. "Where's the temp?"

"I had to send her out to buy paper. We almost ran out. Janet used to look after that sort of thing."

"Well, Janet's retired." Sandra wagged a stern finger at him. "And she's not coming back, so you'd better find someone soon."

"Can't get a secretary, that's the trouble." Malcolm scowled. "They all want to be Executive Assistants."

But Sandra was gone out of earshot.

I don't want an Executive Assistant, he thought as he fiddled disconsolately with his pen. I want Janet . . .

She's not coming back. Sandra was right. And Janet was more than entitled to her retirement after twenty-five dedicated years.

She'd been determined to go. He'd begged her to stay, but she'd long planned to take early retirement. And when entreaties, flattery and outright bribery had fallen on deaf ears, he'd finally had to give in.

"I'll miss you though, Janet. Can't imagine what I'll do without you."

"You'll manage very nicely, Malcolm," she'd said briskly. "You'll soon find a good secretary."

"I'll give you a good reference." Her eyes grew merry.

"Well, if you've enjoyed it that much . . ." He couldn't resist one last effort.

"No, Malcolm." She was adamant. "I'm flattered, really I am, but nobody's indispensable. Besides, I've got big plans for my garden."

Janet always had lots of big plans, between her garden and her church and her relentless fundraising. Malcolm didn't see their attraction himself, and he had occasionally felt a little jealous of their demands on her attention.

Which was ridiculous, he admitted. They never affected her dedication to his business and, besides, how could you be jealous of a bed of lobelias?

Malcolm glanced with amusement at the desk drawer that would hardly open because it was crammed with stacks of useless raffle tickets. Janet was a sort of irresistible force . . . you couldn't say no to her . . .

At least, he'd never been able to. And all he'd ever won was a crocheted toilet roll cover in a violent shade of lilac — which was now in the same drawer as the old tickets.

He chewed his pen, wondering if he'd be any good at raffling whisky and running tombola stalls. Perhaps it would be as fascinating as his business? Perhaps he should give it a try?

He'd never been comfortable with computers and all the modern office paraphernalia. He'd started out in business at the most basic level, with one small tool-hire shop, and it had been fun.

It had also been a huge success — so much so that he'd never really found much time for a personal life. He loved being his own boss, loved working with the staff he regarded as his family, loved planning expansions and new outlets.

But he was still happier with a spanner than a scanner. Office technology made his head buzz.

Janet, a technical wizard, had been his vital right hand. He missed her deeply.

Restless, Malcolm paced his office. Sandra could easily run this business single-handed. If he retired, she'd be free to do just that.

Of course, she'd be reluctant. Sandra's element was negotiations and legal agreements; she was at her happiest with her head buried in a stack of paper. She'd resent having to abandon her office every five minutes to deal with slow deliveries or demanding customers or recalcitrant staff.

But she'd just have to get used to it. Malcolm nodded resolutely at his reflection in the plate-glass window.

The business world was moving on. It was time for him to get off.

SANDRA wouldn't hear of it.

"Don't be daft, Malcolm," she scoffed. "You? Up to your elbows in a herbaceous border? You'd last a week. You'd be bored out of your mind! Anyway, you're far too young to retire, you know."

"You're never too young. And I don't have a totally one-track mind, you know." Malcolm felt rather miffed. "I could do something else besides run this business."

"Oh, I'm sure you could, Malcolm. I just don't think you'd want to." Sandra gave his shoulder a fond squeeze. "You're only out of sorts because of Janet leaving."

"Well, maybe she had the right idea." Malcolm frowned. "Time for a bit of new blood. The modern office makes my head spin. It's outgrown me, Sandra."

Sandra sighed.

"The office isn't the business — it's just the support system. Can you see me sorting out that delivery problem this morning? Or giving the staff a pep-talk? I'd send them to sleep!

"I'd be miserable, and so would they. Come on," she cajoled. "Don't walk out on me, Malcolm."

"Well, I'll have to eventually, and —"

"Oh, eventually. When you've recruited a manager who knows as much about the business as you do — and likes it as much. And when you simply can't live without your herbaceous border any more."

Malcolm couldn't help laughing. "What is a herbaceous border, anyway?"

"That's the spirit. Anyway, retirement's out of the question this financial year."

He frowned.

"Why?"

"I haven't allowed for your gold watch." Sandra smiled. "That's better. Now, let's knock off early. I'll buy you a drink instead."

WITHIN a week, all Malcolm's reservations returned. Sandra had finally insisted he choose a permanent replacement for Janet. She'd even found him the right person, a cousin of her own secretary, Paula.

He had to admit that Paula's cousin was efficient and friendly. She didn't even insist on being his Executive Assistant.

But she wasn't Janet.

She was level headed, but she wasn't a straight-talking, no-nonsense sounding-board for all his ideas. She treated office technology with a familiarity that bordered on contempt, but she couldn't read his mind at nine o'clock in the morning.

"She's marvellous," Malcolm told Sandra. "It's me that's the problem. I'm too set in my ways. I really think . . ."

"Oh, don't start that again," Sandra groaned. "We need you, Malcolm. And what's more, we'd miss you.

"Now tell me, at the risk of getting you on to the subject again, how's Janet enjoying her retirement?"

"I don't know." Malcolm shifted uneasily.

"You don't know?"

"No. It's been so hectic, I just haven't had time to be in touch. I've meant to. I feel bad about it now, but . . ."

"So you should feel bad. You've been going on and on about what a saint Janet Laurie was, and you haven't even bothered to go and see her."

Sandra shook her head sadly.

"You've actually forgotten all about her."

"Certainly not!" Malcolm was flustered.

"Well, I think it's a disgrace! You had us all feeling sorry for you, you were missing her so much. You spent weeks planning her farewell party and agonising over your goodbye speech. Not to mention spending half the profits on flowers and presents."

Sandra was thoroughly enjoying herself.

"And now you've discarded her. Like — like an obsolete typewriter!"

"Sandra!" Malcolm felt his cheeks flush with shame. Joke or no joke, his partner was quite right. He hadn't so much as talked to Janet on the phone.

Not because he hadn't been thinking of her, but because he'd been thinking of her far too much.

"You're absolutely right. I don't know what she must think of me. I'll phone her this minute."

Sandra shook her head and sighed.

"After all this time? I think the least you can do is call by and see her in person. This evening, maybe."

"This evening. Right." Agitated, he turned on his heel and marched into his office, shutting the door firmly.

He didn't see Paula bury her head, laughing, in her hands.

Sandra grinned and winked at her secretary.

"Well, somebody had to get him moving, didn't they?"

Colin Gibson's Almanac
September

WORKING in the woods, among lumberjacks, I learnt a new language.

Do you know what "sneddin" means? Or "barkin and peelin"? Or "cross-cutting the sticks"? Or "burnin the hag"?

As a beginner, I asked a man from Kirriemuir what "sneddin" meant, and it didn't help much when he said it was: "Juist ca'in the doads aff the loags." It meant getting rid of the side branches of a tree just felled.

He gave me a demonstration, moving along a tree-trunk, giving dexterous blows with the axe to right and left, and the branches fell rhythmically away. I never really attained his mastery.

I was much better at "burnin the hag" — lighting a huge bonfire to get rid of all the debris. On a cold September morning, it was a welcome job!

This was a fir wood that was being felled, and I had known it when it was well used by woodcock, wood pigeons and capercaillies.

A lady told me of the time she'd come face to face with one of these birds while on a woodland walk. She'd got a shock when a bird nearly as big as a turkey came charging at her, with a loud rattling in his throat — like pebbles in a can!

She'd realised it was a cock capercaillie, and a very belligerent one, with tail spread, and beak at the ready. When he'd kept advancing, she'd dropped the few wood-anemones she'd picked, turned and ran.

A fortnight later, she ventured to the same spot. All was now peace and quiet, but she soon found what had caused all the disturbance.

Within a few feet of where she had picked the wild flowers was a hollow where the hen capercaillie had had her nest.

Capercaillie.

MALCOLM could have driven, but he was so flustered he felt he needed a brisk walk in the cool evening breeze.

Now, strolling into Janet's tree-lined avenue, his shame turned to apprehension. She might be too busy for surprise guests. Or simply not at home.

As he reached her house his anxiety subsided. Janet was quite clearly at home — and alone.

There she was in her front garden. She had her back to him, so he had

THE LIVET WATER, GRAMPIAN : J CAMPBELL KERR

a moment to smooth his hair and compose himself.

She was reaching up to tie a stray branch of a rambling white rose back on to its trellis. Her hands were sheathed in huge gardening gloves and she was biting her lip as she struggled with a fiddly knot of twine. Her hair was in slight disarray and her cheeks were pink with exertion.

Malcolm's awkwardness dissolved in delight.

"Hello, Janet."

"Malcolm!" She turned and her frown of concentration broke into a welcoming smile. "What a lovely surprise!"

"You look well." Malcolm smiled bashfully back. "I'm sorry I haven't been in touch before."

"No need to be sorry. You've been busy!" Janet peeled off the gauntlets.

"Come in and have some tea? I've just baked a Victoria sponge. I made it for a bring-and-buy sale on Saturday, but I can easily make another . . ."

Malcolm laughed.

"I feel very guilty about the bring-and-buy, but yes, I'd love a cup of tea. It was further than I remembered. Quite a walk."

"I knew you couldn't resist a Victoria sponge," she told him triumphantly. "Have you really walked? Well, it's a lovely evening for it. Come along in."

Janet vanished into the kitchen, and he sat down on a squashy sofa, feeling instantly at home. He'd never been inside her house before, he realised with a faint sense of shock; he'd only ever dropped her off at the door.

"Now, what can I do for you?" Janet reappeared bearing a tea tray with the promised cake.

"Why, nothing at all." Malcolm took his cup. "I just wanted to see how you were getting on. How's retirement?"

Janet laughed. "Non-stop! I can't think why they call it retirement. But great fun.

"You haven't come to drag me back to work, have you?"

She put on an expression of mock horror.

In truth, he'd been tempted to have one last try. If she'd looked bored or aimless, he'd planned to bargain with her for two afternoons a week. It

◀ **p. 118**   ## The River Livet, Grampian

THE River Livet tumbles from the Ladder Hills, in the shadow of the Cairngorms, through Glenlivet, towards the great River Spey.

This is whisky country, where distilleries dot the landscape. Glenlivet has its own malt, and visitors can sample a dram at the distillery.

Grampian is a beautiful area — no wonder the Royal Family love their "holiday home" here — Balmoral Castle!

was obviously out of the question. He sighed inwardly.

"Actually, no."

"Well, now that you put it like that, I shall get all huffy and offended, and ask why not!" Janet laughed.

"I wouldn't dream of dragging you away from your bring-and-buy." Malcolm grinned back. "You're as happy as a sandboy."

"Mm. Thinking of it yourself, are you? Retirement?"

Malcolm shook his head in wonder.

"You can still read my mind, Janet." He took a sip of tea. "I think you've done the right thing. Maybe I should, too."

Janet was silent for a moment as she poured a second cup for them.

D O you really want to retire, Malcolm?"

"No. No, not at all." He met her eyes.

"But I think perhaps I should. I've been married to the business for far too long." For some reason his tongue tripped over the word married.

"Then don't retire. No-one wants you to. Sandra doesn't. The staff don't. And you don't either.

"You're still vital to the business, Malcolm, even —" her mouth twitched "— even if you can't work the fax."

"Ah." Malcolm nodded and grinned. "People have been talking about me behind my back."

"Only because they're all fond of you. Why don't you recruit a manager to take over gradually? You can concentrate on what you enjoy most. And then when you do want to retire — in about a hundred years' time, no doubt — you'll be able to go with a clear conscience."

"Janet, I never could do without your advice!" Malcolm took a deep breath. "But I think, really, I always knew what the solution was.

"The thing is, I've missed you around the office. But it's nothing to do with your typing, or always working late, or how good you are with all those — gadgets. It's just you I've missed.

"You may not be indispensable to the office — but you are to me."

For once Janet was speechless. She set down her cup and stared at him.

"So I don't want you to come back to work. I want you to come to dinner with me. Please, if you'd like to. Tonight. I believe there's an excellent new chef at the Inn on the Green."

Astonished at himself, he held his breath. He'd had no idea that speech was in his head, but now he knew it was why he had really come.

And, even if she told him he was a silly old fool, he wouldn't regret it.

Recovering, Janet smiled and blushed.

"Malcolm, I'd love to."

"I'm glad." He grinned as the weight of his discontent lifted. "Now, why don't I help you wash up these tea things?"

"It's like a late session at the office!" She laughed.

"Well, then, I'll take you up on that! For old times' sake?"

Malcolm smiled at her. He hadn't lost Janet Laurie after all.

"For old times' sake!" □

More Than

SATURDAYS were my favourite day of the week, because Saturday afternoons always meant football, and football meant Grandad, and anything to do with Grandad was fine by me.

I guess we got on so well because we were so much alike. I can remember standing on the terraces with him when I was as young as six years old. I used to copy his every move, shoving my hands deep in my pockets and hunching my shoulders against the biting winter winds, just as he did, and echoing his shouts of encouragement or criticism at the players.

I enjoyed his company so much, and that of his friends, because they all treated me like one of them. At home, Mum and Nan would fuss round me, asking whether I had my gloves, had I been to the toilet; all the usual things.

But as soon as we stepped out of the house, I became a grown-up. When we walked up to our usual spot on the terraces, I would acknowledge our football companions with a nod of my head, and a gruff, "Afternoon," and listen thoughtfully while they discussed whether so-and-so would be playing that day.

Even when I started meeting friends of my own on the steps, I was never ashamed or embarrassed of Grandad, like some of them were about their own relatives.

Grandad was always popular with the youngsters; he spoke intelligently and with knowledge, especially about football, and, as I have said, he always spoke to everyone as if they were an equal.

By the time I reached my teens, our physical likeness was also often commented on, and I didn't mind that either. At just turned sixty, he was still as tall and proud a figure as the one I had seen in his wedding photographs of so many years ago, only his hair seemed to have changed and was now fine and grey.

In some ways, I felt I was more of a son to him than my father. Dad had no time for football, even though Grandad had taken him often to

122

Just A Game

by Faye Robertson

Maggie Palmer.

the ground when he was young.

One of my favourite memories is when we came home late one evening, like two naughty schoolboys, having joined Grandad's friends down at the local men's working club. Grandad had smuggled me in and I had sat with them all, feeling extremely grown-up. But I was soon reduced to my proper state when Mum sent me upstairs to get changed for tea, and Nan began to scold Grandad.

"I don't know what you think you were doing, Len, for goodness' sake, taking a child into that place, really I don't!"

"Ah, no harm was done, Jessie, don't make such a fuss," he had replied, looking up to give me a wink as I peered over the bannisters.

I had fled up to my bedroom before I could giggle, aware from that point on that we somehow shared a secret that no-one else was party to.

It had always been the two of us, and, at thirteen, I could see us still standing on the terrace steps for years to come, drinking our beef tea and shouting encouragement.

Perhaps that's why it came as such a shock to me when he died so suddenly.

IT came as a shock to all of us, of course, but even so, I knew that Mum and Dad were very worried about me. I walked around for months afterwards like a zombie. I ate very little, slept even less but, most worrying for them of all, I didn't go to one football game.

We all knew why. Football had become synonymous with Grandad and, although I knew I was just fooling myself, I somehow felt that, once I stood on that terrace alone, it would be a final seal on what had happened. I would finally understand that he wasn't coming back.

So, I didn't go. I spent Saturday afternoons shopping with Mum and Dad, or in my room, listening to music. I couldn't even bring myself to listen to the results on the radio.

Nan had informed Dad that she still wanted to live in her own home for as long as she was able and, as we only lived around the corner, he accepted that with little comment. She came to visit quite often, though, and it was on one of these Saturday morning visits that Mum and Dad left me alone with her, to talk.

I had seen her a few times since Grandad died, and I had hugged her and told her how sorry I was, but I could see in her eyes that she knew I had not accepted what had happened.

"How are you, Jack?" she asked me, ruffling my hair in the way she had always done.

"OK," I said, moving my head away as usual.

"Your dad told me that you haven't been back to the ground since your grandad passed away." She surveyed me thoughtfully.

"I can't go without him," I said flatly. "It would be like having the Queen's speech on Christmas Day without the Queen." I swallowed painfully.

She smiled a little sadly.

"I know what you mean. I see him everywhere. I was hanging out the washing yesterday when I saw a fox watching me from under the hedge. I went to run indoors to tell him . . . Then I realised he wouldn't be there." Her eyes filled with tears. "I don't know if I can go on without him, Jack."

I took her hand, a lump in my throat, my own eyes stinging as I fought not to cry.

"Don't say that, Nan. I know what you mean, but you can't give up. He wouldn't have wanted that."

My voice faded slowly away. She was watching me, the tears genuine, but she smiled through them at my words.

"Yes, Jack, I'm glad you realise that," she said softly, reaching out a hand to wipe away the tear that had finally broken loose and was trailing down my cheek. "We all have to go on."

She turned to where she had left her handbag by the side of her chair, and lifted it on to her lap.

"I have something for you here." I watched as she pulled out a small bundle of purple and blue and placed it on my lap. "He would have wanted you to have it."

I stared at it for a few moments, then carefully unravelled its length. It was a scarf in the colours of our football team, hand-knitted by my Nan when she was only a teenager. Grandad had worn it to every match he had ever attended.

I looked up at her in disbelief.

"I can't take this!" I said finally. "It was his most treasured possession! You must keep it, Nan, not me."

"No, you're wrong, Jack," she urged, pushing it back towards me. "How do you think he would feel, knowing that you had deserted the team? Football was his life, his one true passion. He was thrilled when you took to the game, especially as your father wasn't really interested. He once said he thought of you as his real heir." Her eyes were kind as she looked at me.

"Did he really say that?" My voice was choked.

"Absolutely. That's not to say he didn't care for your father, of course. Peter was his only son and he loved him very much. But I know he felt closer to you. You understood each other. You mustn't lose that, Jack. That would be unfair to him."

I buried my face in the purple and blue wool. Could I do it? Could I really go back to the ground without him? I couldn't bear the thought of standing on the terrace with the yawning empty space beside me. Outside the football ground I could fill the void with other people, other voices. But inside, only Grandad would fit the gap and I didn't know if I could bear to not have him there.

But, looking up at my nan, I knew I had to try. I knew that it was what he would have wanted.

A FEW hours later, I stood with my hands on the rail in front of me, surveying the ground. Nothing appeared to have changed since the last time we had been there. The players were warming up, while the supporters got their tea and made their way down the steps to their own particular spot.

I stood stiffly, my hands jammed into my pockets, the purple and blue scarf wound around my neck feeling strangely alien inside my jacket. I was standing in our usual place, on the tenth step up, to the left of the goal.

On the way to the ground I had decided to go into the stand instead, as having a seat would make such a change to how we normally spent a match. Most of the grounds were already all-seater stadiums, but our little ground still had three sides standing room only.

However, when I came to buy my ticket, I found my legs wandering of their own accord over to our usual end and, as I took my stance on the red railings, I knew I could stand in no other place.

The team, having gone to take off their tracksuits, ran out to the club song and I clapped with the rest of the fans, then leaned forward as the whistle blew and the game commenced. It was cold, and the sun was very bright.

I CLOSED my eyes, a sudden wave of anguish sweeping over me. How could I have thought I was strong enough to come here by myself? As the crowd cheered and shouted, the pain of Grandad's absence was almost too much to bear. I could feel the space next to me as if I had had some piece of me physically removed. I clenched my hands and gritted my teeth, refusing to cry in public.

I was so lonely, I missed him so much.

It was then that I felt it. A presence next to me, so light and ethereal that I could easily have imagined it. I kept my eyes closed, holding my breath. The smell of beef tea filled the air and from beside me came the sound of someone breathing on their hands to warm them up.

"Dodgy tackle, eh, Grandad?" I said softly, straining my ears to catch a reply. Was that a chuckle, lost in the wind?

I opened my eyes. There was no-one beside me, or even particularly close to me, but I still had the feeling that I was not alone. I pulled the scarf tightly around my neck.

"I'm wearing it now, Grandad," I whispered, knowing that he had heard.

I was finally aware of what my nan had been trying to tell me. I had thought that coming to the football match would be like saying goodbye and I would finally lose Grandad forever. But I was so wrong.

I could hear his voice now, quoting Bill Shankly: "Football's not a matter of life and death, Jack — it's much more important than that!" His voice held more than a hint of amusement.

It had been his greatest passion in life, and if I ever wanted to find him, I finally realised, then this was where he would be. ☐

IN HER TRUE Colours

by Patti Hales

GOODNESS, but it was windy! Pursing her lips, Jane Wishart attempted to blow a long, waving lock of hair out of her eyes as she struggled to open the front door. A pointless exercise, she conceded silently, as the strands resettled themselves over her line of vision.

Once indoors, she shrugged out of her beige mackintosh and hung it on the peg beside her grey jacket and best navy coat, then she slid her briefcase into the small cupboard under the stairs.

She wouldn't need it for a whole week. Thank heavens for half-term holidays, she thought, kicking off her shoes and pushing her feet into her comfortable slippers. Utter bliss!

Tea. That was

Caldwell.

what she needed now! A good strong cuppa and a sit-down to recover from her battle against the elements. In the kitchen she flicked the switch on the kettle with one hand; with the other she searched her greying hair for a pin to secure the offending lock.

"You'd look years younger if you'd have that lot cut into a modern style." Her sister, Hazel's, words from the week before sprang suddenly into Jane's mind. "Heaven's, you're only in your fifties," Hazel had carried on, "and it's gorgeous hair. I've always envied you for having it."

Hazel had envied her? That revelation had come as a surprise to Jane. As far as she was concerned, the boot was firmly on the other foot!

"Chalk and cheese, my girls," their mother had been fond of saying. "One with beauty, one with brains."

Hazel had always been the pretty one. She'd sparkled in pink floral frocks with long ribbon sashes, while Jane had been kitted out in more sombre navys and dark greens.

And when it came to confidence . . . Hazel had been blessed with the ability to grab at what she wanted with both hands and see it through without wavering. It had only been in later life that Jane had found the courage to speak out if she felt that something wasn't as it should be.

Sighing deeply, Jane forced herself to remember what else Hazel had said. It came to her immediately.

"You should have a bit of colour put in it, too." Her sister had patted her own smooth head which was still the same golden blonde as it had always been.

"Remember how it used to be? That glorious flame red?" She stopped for a moment, looking at Jane as if she was a specimen under a microscope. Then — "Honestly, your face is screaming out for a bit of colour!"

"You're not seriously suggesting that I dye my hair, are you?"

Hazel giggled. "That's exactly what I'm suggesting."

As she waited for the tea to brew, Jane studied her reflection in the small mirror she kept on the window ledge. A pale face stared back at her: light brown eyes, neat, regular features . . . colourless skin and, yes, matching, colourless hair.

A beige person, she decided. A nondescript, neutral human being!

Perhaps . . . she wondered for a moment, then scolded herself mentally.

Her hair was fine as it was. Besides, it suited the clothes she wore every day, whether she was working or not. The good-quality tweed skirts and the plain matching jumpers and cardigans had earned her the not-too-flattering nickname of Tyrant in a Twinset — a nickname that had been in use for more years than she cared to remember.

When she'd first heard it being bandied around the playground, she'd been hurt. Somehow she'd managed to laugh it off by saying that it gave her an air of authority . . . something several of the younger teachers didn't seem to possess, she'd added silently.

And nothing had changed, Jane thought as she carried her cup of tea and a couple of digestive biscuits into the living-room and settled herself

In Her True Colours

into a deep armchair, overlooking the garden.

Take Justin Solley, for instance. Did he really look like a teacher? No, she decided for the umpteenth time, he didn't. Not with his long hair and the way he lolloped around the place like a gangly red setter puppy. His classes were noisy and he allowed his six-year-olds to read comics.

Not only allowed, but actively encouraged it!

And, although she'd instructed herself to mind her own business, her tongue had got the better of her.

"I honestly don't think —" she had started to point out, but had been swiftly interrupted.

"Jane, my sweetheart —" she'd flinched when Justin had said that, felt her cheeks colour as he'd carried on "— it gets them reading, because they can't wait to find out what's going to happen next.

"Of course it doesn't work for all of them — some still need to be taught the old way — but what we must remember is that kids are individuals, too. We adults don't have the monopoly on that and we can't lump them all in the same category and expect instant results.

"They're growing up in a rapidly changing world, Jane. They need to be able to cope with choices. If we forget that, then we're selling them short."

Choices were all very well, she'd thought, but there were other things to be taken into consideration.

"What about discipline?" she'd asked. "If we don't teach them that, then aren't we selling them short in another way?"

She'd felt her forehead form itself into deep grooves, her mouth tighten, but Justin had smiled gently.

"There's dictated discipline and there's self-discipline. I know which I prefer," he'd said quietly.

PUT that way, she'd no real argument to offer, and had to accept that Justin's methods not only worked, but that his pupils worshipped the ground his trainer-clad feet trod.

Another incident she'd recently experienced sprang into Jane's mind. It had been with Sharon Lewis, who taught the reception class.

Sharon had a swinging ponytail hairdo, wore garishly-coloured trousers and sat on the floor a lot. Sometimes she even brought in her guitar and the results could be heard echoing round the old building.

That in itself was bad enough, in Jane's opinion, but after her talk with Justin she had kept her mouth firmly shut . . . until the morning when a tiny girl had turned up wearing red lipstick and vivid green eyeshadow.

She'd looked like a little clown and Jane's hands had itched to get hold of the child and march her off to the staff room to wash it all off immediately — the way any sensible teacher would have done in the old days.

But Sharon . . . she'd just laughed and, by lunchtime, the rest of her group had been made-up to look like circus clowns while the classroom had been transformed into a Big Top.

Later, when Jane, unable to keep her thoughts to herself any longer, had questioned Sharon as to the purpose behind her methods, the young woman had grinned.

"Jane, this is the Nineties. These children have to be armed with a lot more than the basics to survive in the big bad world. They have to know how to look the part as well as be trained for it. A bit of imagination can be the difference between getting a job . . . or being stuck in the dole queue."

Remembering that particular point, Jane reflected on her own life. She curled her legs up underneath her and let her memory wander back.

Had she really wanted to be a school teacher? Or had she simply fallen into it, because someone — her father, probably — had ordained that's how it should be?

It wasn't that she hated her job, she didn't, but supposing she'd wanted to be an author? Or a top class chef? Would she have had the courage to come straight out and say so?

She doubted it. Coward, she told herself.

Hazel would have rebelled. Kicked up a terrible fuss and, regardless, would have followed her instincts, which had been to go into fashion, starting at the bottom as a sales junior and working her way up to a top buyer.

Jane's mouth twisted into a wry smile. Poor Hazel. How awful it must be for her to have a sister who was one of life's fashion failures! It must be like a hairdresser sitting behind someone with split ends or a bad perm, and itching to pull out her scissors and get to work.

And really, young Sharon did have a point about looking the part. Only last week there had been an article in one of the newspapers about how beautiful women and handsome men had an immediate advantage over less attractive people when it came to job interviews.

Style mattered these days, it seemed.

Deep in thought, Jane reached for her cup, but the first tepid sip told her she'd spent far too long day-dreaming. Her eyes strayed out to her garden. It was screaming out for attention, she thought, looking at the too-long grass which was due for its last cut before the winter months set in with a vengeance.

Well, she had the time now. Nine whole days, counting the two weekends.

Leaning over, she switched on the television and tried to concentrate on the six o'clock news. Such doom and gloom, she thought sadly, almost relieved when it came to an end, to be replaced with a cheerful-looking weather forecaster, predicting confidently that the wind would drop and tomorrow would be dry with long sunny spells.

"Good," she said, out loud, making a mental list.

Shopping, first thing. Followed by a trip to the library . . . coffee and a sandwich . . . then she'd be ready to get stuck into the large lawn.

Mr Sinclair, who lived next door, had kindly offered to cut it when he did his own, but she'd politely turned down his offer.

Colin Gibson's Almanac

October

I'VE always found that cats are very independent. Out and about, dogs leave the choice of routes to their masters. But not cats — they go their own way.

Many farms have a number of cats leading unofficial lives around the premises. They form a floating population in the summer months and in winter take up their abode in barns and sheds. They are more or less self-supporting, and are useful in keeping mice, rats and rabbits in check.

At such farms, only one cat is usually allowed inside the house, and that cat will bar the way — fangs bared, back raised, every hair bristling — if any other cat tries to enter.

Even well-fed house cats can't always refrain from stalking small birds and mice. Yet my own cat, Blackie, never touches the garden birds. When he was young, I told him they were my "hens," and to be left severely alone. He has always respected that order.

Cats eat some strange things at times. One was noticed in a garden eating peas in the pod, and another had a taste for cauliflowers!

Instinctive hunters some of them may be, but they have a gentler side and make good foster mothers. Even orphan hares and rabbits have been cared for by cats, and one cat even mothered a chicken!

I suppose the tortoiseshell would be regarded as the loveliest of cats, but it cannot be denied that a cat, whether black, white, sandy-coloured or striped, gives a pleasing homely look to the fireside — especially when the October evenings are drawing in, and dusk so quickly gives way to dark.

"It gives me a bit of exercise," she'd told him, admitting to herself that she was telling a rather large fib, because it would have been nice to have one job less to cope with after a busy and demanding week.

"You're hopeless, Jane," Hazel had groaned when Jane had admitted what she'd done. "Absolutely off your rocker."

"I can manage by myself." Jane's response had been delivered through stiff lips.

"You and your precious pride!" Hazel hit back. "He's a lovely man, handsome, a widower." Grinning, she ticked the words off on her fingers. "Not too old, nice bungalow, smart car. What woman in her right mind would turn him down?"

"This one!" Jane had turned away as hot colour rushed over her cheeks. Mr Sinclair was everything Hazel had said. A lovely man.

THE following afternoon she knelt on the grass and squirted oil into her old lawnmower. "Drat!" The can developed a will of its own and a greasy puddle stared up at her from the lap of her tweed skirt, while a trickle of thick slime dripped off the sleeve of her old brown cardigan.

"If you don't mind me saying so, you're not wearing the right clothes for gardening."

Jane looked up in the direction of the clear voice. A girl, about nine or ten, she reckoned, was perched between the thick branches of Mr Sinclair's old apple tree.

"What on earth are you doing up there?" she asked.

The child tossed back her long, red curls.

"Watching you." She shifted position, so that her thin legs dangled above Jane's head. "And wondering why you're playing with oil when you're wearing your best clothes."

Impudent little monkey! Jane squared her shoulders.

"These are not my best clothes."

"Well, if you say so. But I still think you'd be more comfortable wearing your old jeans . . . you know . . . like a proper gardener?"

Clothes maketh not the man. The old expression sprang to Jane's lips, but she bit back the words. Not only would they sound old fashioned, but the child, whoever she was, did have a point.

A skirt — and stockings, through which the dampness from the grass was seeping into her knees — were not exactly practical attire for the task in hand.

"What's your name?" she asked instead.

There was a rustle of dead leaves as the slight figure dropped out of the tree and on to the lawn.

"Briony. What's yours?"

"Miss Wishart." Janet stressed the Miss.

"Ah." The freckled nose wrinkled. "Miss Wishart. Now I know why you're dressed like that. You're one of these career girls, aren't you? A power dresser, that's what it's called.

"I've read about career girls. I think I might like to be one, too. I don't want to get married, you see." She looked round her and lowered her voice.

"I think boys are awful, but you won't tell Grandad, will you? I mean he's a boy and he's lovely. It's just some of the others . . ."

Grandad? Of course. She should have known who the child was. Jane suddenly realised she knew very little about her next door neighbour, who was striding across the lawn, tall and elegant in brown cord trousers and a cream shirt.

"Briony, you're not bothering Miss Wishart, are you?" Mr Sinclair's smile was guarded. "My granddaughter has a rather mobile tongue, I'm afraid."

"I certainly have not!" Briony's cheeks were scarlet with indignation. "I'm just honest to a fault, Mum says."

Brown eyes narrowed — kind eyes, Jane thought — as Mr Sinclair ruffled the mass of ginger curls which reminded her so much of her own hair at the same age.

"There's a little thing called tact, darling," Mr Sinclair said.

Briony raised her eyes heavenwards.

"Grandad, tact can be another word for a lie, you know. Like saying you love your best friend's new jumper, when secretly you think it's the most horrible thing in the whole world." She looked at Jane. "That's true, isn't it?"

Jane nodded. Whoever was teaching this child, was doing a great job. Probably someone like Justin Solley with his undying faith in honesty between the generations.

Then it struck her. Hazel was the only one who was ever completely honest with her. Justin had been tactful and Sharon, too. Instead of telling Jane what was really inside their heads — that she ought to be considering new ways herself — they'd merely skimmed the surface so as not to offend her.

How awful! Tyrant in a Twinset took on a whole new meaning. People were scared of her! Even Mr Sinclair, judging by his uncomfortable expression. All of them, except Hazel and . . .

SHE cleared her throat.

"So are you spending the whole day with your grandad, Briony?"

"The whole week. Mum's pregnant, you see, and there have been a few problems, so they've taken her into hospital to monitor the situation."

So calm. So knowledgeable. Jane smiled. "I'm sure everything will be all right."

"It will be. The scan was fine. This time next week I should have a new sister. Or a brother, I suppose. Thank goodness I've got Grandad to take care of me. I'd be really lonely without him."

Over the child's head Mr Sinclair looked at Janet.

"I was wondering . . ." He stopped. "No, it doesn't matter . . ."

"Grandad," Briony encouraged. "Go on. Ask her."

"Yes, ask me." Was that really her talking, Jane wondered as she waited. Mr Sinclair's colour deepened.

"She wants to go shopping. For clothes and things, and I'm afraid that I'm not very good at that sort of thing."

"So I asked him who lived next door and he said a very nice lady," Briony explained cheerfully. "Then I said perhaps she — you, I mean — would come shopping with me instead and then he said —"

Jane wasn't sure she really wanted to hear what he'd said. It would probably be tactful, anyway.

"I'd love to, Briony," she told the child.

Later that evening, Jane struggled to concentrate on the television, her mind elsewhere. What had she let herself in for?

A car boot sale — she'd never been to one of these — tomorrow, after church. The cinema on Tuesday to see the newest Disney film and, of

Loch Leven.

course, the shopping expedition.

It had all happened so quickly!

Mr Sinclair — Leonard — had insisted on cutting the lawn while his granddaughter helped his neighbour to bake a quick cake. Then they'd all sat in Jane's sun parlour and played several riotous games of Snap.

Briony had been the outright winner. She was quick. And smart, too, Jane thought. Not just at cards, but in her general observations.

"When we go to town, I'd like to have my hair trimmed," she'd said, looking sideways at Jane.

"Have you ever thought about having yours cut short? It would look really great! And you could have some lowlights put in it. They're like highlights, only different!"

Highlights? Lowlights? Baffled and at a loss for words, Jane could only nod vaguely, but the next moment had found herself eagerly agreeing to try on some comfy trousers and a jumper in a bright colour.

Morning Meditation

THE day is soft and golden,
  There's dew upon the leaves,
Wild flowers peppered in the grass
  Nod in the gentle breeze.
The air is filled with birdsong
  As thrushes start to sing,
And overhead in skies of blue
  Are swallows on the wing.
And all along the river
  The willows bend and sway
In wind that stirs the water
  Where sunbeams dance and play.

And swans with downy wings are
  Serenely gliding by,
Their feathers are unruffled
  And heads are held up high.
These poised and graceful creatures
  Are soft and snowy white —
A vision of tranquillity
  All bathed in morning light.
And all around is beauty
  In everything I see,
For all of nature seems to blend
  In perfect harmony.
      — *Kathleen Gillum.*

Gordon Henderson.

A dress too. And a winter coat.

"You're sure you don't mind traipsing round a field looking at other people's junk?" Leonard had asked as they'd left.

"I'm looking forward to it," Jane had assured him, realising it was the truth.

Giving up on the television, she went upstairs and ran a deep bath. Soaking in the scented foam which she kept for high days and holidays, she mentally scanned the contents of her wardrobe.

Absolutely colourless, she thought. Except perhaps for a bright scarf or two. Well, it would have to do, for tomorrow anyway.

Then, anything could happen. From Tyrant in a Twinset to something more fitting for a teacher of the Nineties, who would always insist on good ground rules, but who could also appreciate the need for change.

Jane let her toes play through the scented bubbles. Lady in Red? Yes, that might be nice! □

The Music In Her Heart

by Shirley Worrall

GAIL'S day started perfectly. Peter rang, just as she was leaving for the office.

"I've managed to get four tickets for the concert. Shall I ring Tom and Melanie and see if they're still keen to go?"

"Yes, do." Gail was delighted.

They'd seen the notices for the concert, decided they had to go, then learnt that all tickets were sold. Peter's brother worked for the local radio station, however, where several complimentary tickets were always sent, and their luck was in.

"I'll call for you at seven," Peter said. "We'll go for a meal afterwards, shall we?"

"It sounds perfect."

There was a dreamy silence.

"See you later, then," Peter said softly.

The brief call was an unexpected bonus on a Friday morning and, instead of taking the bus to work, she decided to walk. The autumn sun shone and the leaves glowed like polished gold.

She and Peter had been seeing each other for three months. He'd started calling at the estate agent's where Gail worked, looking for a small, easily manageable property suitable for his grandparents. They'd bumped into each other in town a couple of times, chatted about the property market and his grandparents, and Peter had asked her out.

Now, they were seeing a lot of each other and Gail was content.

Her morning in the estate agent's was busy, but she felt on top of the world. She enjoyed her work, got on well with her colleagues and, better still, she would be going to the concert with Peter.

She smiled to herself, realising they had no idea what they'd be hearing. The promotional posters had mentioned two names and "additional artists". For all they knew, the "additional artists" could be awful.

She didn't care.

The concert was to celebrate the overdue opening of the town's new concert hall. The thrill was attending the very first concert. It didn't matter what they heard.

Gail went window shopping in her lunch hour. There was a spring in her step and a warmth in her heart.

Suddenly, though, in just a

Behrens.

split-second, all the joy in her day vanished.

She was about to walk into the newsagent's when she spotted a man on the other side of the road. His back was to her so she couldn't see his face, but the way he walked, the long, easy stride, the way his fair hair caught the sun . . . he looked exactly like Richard.

Gail forgot the magazine she'd intended to buy. Instead, she walked slowly back to the office.

It wasn't the first time she'd spotted a complete stranger and been reminded of Richard. It probably wouldn't be the last, either. It had been four years since she'd seen him. Four years, and still the sight of a stranger could bring it all back to her.

Sitting in front of her computer that afternoon, she remembered the first time she saw him.

She was twenty-one, attending a friend's twenty-first. Jenny, the birthday girl, had persuaded her brother and a few of his friends to provide the musical entertainment.

Richard played the guitar.

They got chatting, he asked her out, and later she discovered that he also played piano, violin and saxophone. He came from a large family, three sisters and two brothers, and every member of the family, including their parents, seemed capable of playing at least six instruments.

As an only child, Gail found it amazing. In Richard's house, there was never silence. Someone was always practising this, or attempting that, and, before long, the whole family had joined in.

Gail's talents as a musician had started and ended at primary school, when she'd been allowed to hit the cymbals at what everyone hoped would be an appropriate moment.

IT took less than a month to fall hopelessly in love with him. They were together for two years — the happiest years of Gail's life. Richard had just graduated from a music course at college and was working at his father's firm temporarily. Gail often thought he didn't feel fully dressed unless he had a musical instrument at his fingertips.

His dream came true when he was invited, courtesy of a friend of his father's, to attend an audition — in Paris. The audition took place on Gail's twenty-third birthday.

She spent half the day hoping he wouldn't get it, and the other half hating herself for such terrible thoughts.

He rang in the evening.

"I hate being away from you on your birthday," he said.

"It doesn't matter. The flowers made up for it. They're lovely. Thank you." But the flowers hadn't made up for his absence.

"I'll be home tomorrow and we'll go somewhere special to celebrate." He sounded genuinely unhappy. "Fancy me being stuck in Paris, the city of romance, on your birthday. We should be walking hand-in-hand, gazing at the Eiffel Tower."

"How did the audition go?" She hardly dared to ask.

"It could have been better," he said, "but then again, I suppose it could have been a lot worse. I don't know, Gail, we'll have to wait and see."

"Fingers crossed then," she said.

"And toes." He spoke lightly, as if it wouldn't be the end of his world if he failed the audition. "Anyway, I'll see you tomorrow. About sixish. I'm counting the minutes. Paris is — I don't know, lonely somehow. Or perhaps it's just me. I love you, Gail."

"I love you, too . . ."

Things went wrong from that moment on.

Richard came back, but the tension of having to wait before he heard one way or the other made him edgy. He wanted to discuss what would happen if he was accepted and joined the orchestra, but he was also

138

frightened to plan ahead in case he wasn't successful.

When the letter arrived from Paris, they were barely speaking. Things were so bad that Richard handed her the letter without a word. They were standing in Gail's kitchen and she read the letter, folded it and returned it to the envelope.

She felt as if her life was over.

"Congratulations." Tears filled her eyes.

"Congratulations?" He stuffed the envelope in his jacket pocket. "On what? Look at us, Gail. What's happening to us?"

"You're about to embark on a dazzling career," she answered quietly.

"I wouldn't even have considered it if I'd known you were so set against it."

"It's not a case of being against it, Richard. I can't go, and you know it. I can't leave Mum and Dad, not now. All these tests Dad's having — the more tests he has, the more likely it seems that he'll need heart surgery. I don't think he has any choice."

"I know, Gail, but —"

"No, Richard, you don't know. Mum's worried to death. So am I, if I'm honest. What if something were to happen to Dad? I'm all she's got."

"Credit me with some intelligence, Gail. I know that. I know how worrying it is." He clasped her hands in his and spoke more calmly. "But it's only Paris. We'd be at the end of a phone. We could be here in no time."

"For how long? A day? Two days? A week perhaps? Long enough to pat her on the back and tell her she has to worry alone?"

"And you don't know that we'd be in Paris. You said yourself that a lot of travelling was involved."

"But we'd work something out. You can't live your life by what might happen, Gail."

"I'm not coming, Richard."

They argued for hours, but Gail knew it was over. If she'd had brothers or sisters, things would have been very different, but she was all her parents had. She couldn't leave them.

"Then I won't go." Richard threw himself down on to a chair.

"Don't be ridiculous."

"Who's being ridiculous? It would be more ridiculous if I went without you. It's simple, Gail, if you don't go, I don't go. I won't go alone."

"You have to," Gail said calmly. "This means more to you than anything —"

"No! You mean more to me than anything."

"At the moment, perhaps. In a few years, though, what then? You'd resent me. You'd think of the career you might have had, and you'd resent me. You'd grow to hate me."

"I could never hate you," he scoffed.

"Richard," she spoke as calmly as she could, "you have to go, I have to stay."

A DOZEN letters arrived, but Gail tore them up into pieces so tiny that she wouldn't have been able to read them even if she'd wanted to.

Her dad, as they'd guessed, had surgery, and there were complications. His recovery took a lot longer than they'd expected, but at least he had recovered.

Gail had a lot to occupy her mind, but it didn't stop her spending every waking moment thinking of Richard.

In the last four years her only unimagined reminder of him had been the two occasions she'd bumped into his mother.

"How's Richard?" Gail asked, when they'd spent a couple of awkward minutes discussing the weather.

"Fine. We had a week in Paris with him before Christmas."

"Is he —" Gail had been about to ask if he was happy, but she couldn't. "Busy?" she asked instead.

"Very." And they'd quickly changed the subject.

On the second occasion, Gail learnt that Richard's parents had spent two weeks with him in Paris because he hadn't been able to find time to come home, that his career had really taken off, that he was orchestra leader, and that he was setting off for New York.

That was her only reminder of the love they'd shared — that and seeing at least half a million people who looked exactly like him . . .

* * * *

"Are you spending the night?" Julie asked with a laugh.

Gail came to with a start, realising it was after five.

"I was miles away." She smiled self-consciously and switched off her computer.

She walked home instead of taking the bus — not because she wanted to savour the joy of the day, but because she was so depressed she wanted to be alone.

The evening ahead had been something to look forward to. Now, her head was throbbing and she was dreading it. She would have to listen to music that she'd probably heard Richard play . . .

For Peter, Tom and Melanie's sake, she put on a bright smile, and

Clapham, North Yorkshire

NORTH Yorkshire is the largest English county and contains two national parks. It's an unspoilt area, well known for its peace and quiet.

Clapham, which is west of Harrogate, is a popular centre for walking and climbing. Nearby, waterfalls and limestone caves filled with stalagmites and stalactites attract many visitors.

CLAPHAM, NORTH YORKSHIRE : J CAMPBELL KERR

"oohed" and "aahed" at the luxurious concert hall, but her headache was getting worse by the minute.

When she opened the souvenir programme, Richard's name leapt off the page. It hadn't been a stranger at all. It really had been Richard. At that moment, they were in the same building. She'd assumed they were miles apart, countries apart even, but he was in the same country, the same town, the same building. Any minute now —

She couldn't stay to watch. According to the programme, he was playing one of his own compositions. She couldn't sit and listen to it — watch him play.

She opened her mouth to utter an excuse, say she felt sick or faint, which she did, but Peter clasped her cold hand in his and she had to give him a bright smile.

She would have liked nothing better than to go home, but she couldn't spoil his evening just because she didn't think she could cope with watching an ex-boyfriend play the piano for a few minutes.

"I'll be fine," she said.

"You're glad you came, aren't you?"

"Of course." She gave him her brightest smile. "I wouldn't have missed it for anything."

The lights dimmed and Richard was introduced as a local boy made good. Gail heard every word, but when Richard walked on stage, she lost sight of everything else. Part of her had hoped he might look old, less attractive, but he looked exactly as he had four years ago.

Afterwards, she couldn't remember what he'd said to the audience and she didn't have a clue what he'd played.

The evening finally came to an end and Peter drove Gail home.

There was no point in letting things continue. She'd known it from the moment she'd looked across the road that morning and seen the man she'd assumed was a stranger.

In four years, she'd had three relationships. First had been Michael. That had fizzled out after a couple of months. Then came Douglas. She'd ended things on Richard's birthday, having spent the entire day wondering what he was doing, where he was spending his birthday, and who was with him. Then Peter . . .

The trouble was, she was beginning to doubt that anyone would make her feel the way Richard had.

She invited Peter in, and tried to give him a gentle explanation of her feelings.

"But things are great, Gail," he protested. "We're great together."

Peter didn't understand and she couldn't blame him. It had been four years. Four years and she was no nearer getting over Richard than she had been three years and eleven months ago.

When he'd gone, Gail threw herself down on her bed and burst into tears. Sleep refused to come and she lay for hours, her thoughts in turmoil.

When morning came, her head throbbed, her throat was painful, and her eyes were red and sore.

She had to get out. Putting on her coat, she left her flat and walked.

She wanted to clear her head, but all she could do was speculate on Richard's life. He didn't look as if he'd changed at all, but how could she tell?

Perhaps he was married to someone who shared his love of music, someone who could play fifteen instruments brilliantly, someone who could teach their children to play fifteen instruments brilliantly.

She sat by the lake in the park, watching the ducks and trying to get Richard off her mind. It no longer mattered. Rightly or wrongly, she'd sent him away. Things had turned out well for her father, but would her mother have coped alone? At the time, she'd made the only choice she could.

DUSK was settling on the town when she walked slowly back to her flat. Her flat came into view and her heart began pounding. It looked like — but she didn't trust her judgement any more.

Only when she reached the foot of the steps did she believe it. Richard was sitting on the top step, leaning against the railings — and he was asleep.

She stood completely still, unable to move. She must have stood there for half an hour, but it was getting dark and cold. She reached out a trembling hand and gave his shoulder a gentle shake.

Suddenly he looked wide awake and Gail took a backwards step.

"Hello, Richard. How have you been?" Did she really say that?

"Fine." He stood up and brushed the dust from his jeans and jacket. "You?"

"Oh, yes. Fine."

"Did you come to see me?" Why else would he be there? And the prospect had held so much meaning for him that he'd fallen asleep! "Would you like a coffee?"

"Thanks, that would be good."

She poured their coffee. They ignored the seats, preferring to stand.

"I saw you play last night," she said.

"Did you? Did you like it?"

"Yes." She flushed. "Actually, I was so surprised that you were there, I can't remember what you played."

He smiled at her honesty.

"It was a bit touch and go whether I was there or not. However, I got back yesterday morning, came into town for a quick run through, went home and slept, played at the concert, went home and slept, and came to see you."

"And slept," she added quietly.

"Sorry." He smiled ruefully. "It's probably jet-lag or something. I was in Australia on Tuesday."

If Looks Could Kill. . .

IF Anne or I are not down at our local shop before Charlie the postman leaves for his round to the Riggin, he picks up our daily paper and brings it with him.

Anne's the one who gets to it first, to cast her eye down the births, marriages and deaths.

I came into breakfast one morning to find her immersed in the paper.

"John, Mrs Berwick has died."

Dear old Mrs Berwick. I must tell you what I did one morning on her behalf.

Anne and I were in Crail one Saturday morning when a car drew up beside us.

It was Nora, Mrs Berwick's daughter, a farmer's wife we both knew well and liked.

She was just going to choose some curtain material and then have a cup of tea with her mum.

Would Anne come and help her choose the material, and then go with her to see her mum? Anne said, "yes" to both. As she was leaving to go with Nora on the curtain choosing, she turned to me.

"John, go and buy a box of chocolates. We can't go empty handed," she whispered.

Now, I ask you, what did dear old Mrs Berwick want with a box of chocolates? I bet she would just put them in a cupboard, like Anne does.

I saw a butcher's nearby and went in and bought two of this season's lamb chops, and got the butcher to wrap them up in brown paper.

I waited for the women to return, complete with their material.

"John, have you got a present?" Anne asked quietly.

"Yes, dear." No mention that it wasn't a box of chocolates.

When we got to Mrs Berwick's cottage, she said how pleased she was to see us.

I handed over "our" present.

When the old lady opened it, you should have seen Anne's face. If looks could kill, I would have been dead on the spot.

Mrs Berwick was no fool by anyone's standards and must have seen Anne's face and guessed it was me who had done the shopping.

"Oh, John, how kind of you. They will do my dinner." She was one of the old school; dinner meant her meal at midday.

The Farmer And His Wife

Four years apart and they suddenly had nothing to say to each other. They both sipped at coffee that was too hot to swallow. Gail had a dozen questions, but she didn't ask a single one.

"How's your dad?" he finally asked.

"Fine. He has to take it easy, but he's fine."

"And your mum?"

"She's still the same. Bossing him, worrying about him." She smiled.

"Last night —" Richard spoke softly "— was the last time I'll play in public."

Gail thought he must surely hear her heart pounding.

144

I could see she was really pleased. And, would you believe it, the old soul rang us that night to say how much she had enjoyed the chops.

I had to smile. They'd obviously been a far better gift than a box of chocolates!

Thinking of presents, my mother was, to put it mildly, the most difficult person to please. The fact that she didn't approve of my Anne didn't help matters.

You won't believe this, but Anne was never over our farmhouse doorstep until after we were married.

Dad got over his present problem at Christmas and Mum's birthday by telling her to go and choose something and he would pay. Poor Dad, sometimes she made him pay dearly!

One year, when she was near eighty, Anne bought her a beautiful large mohair scarf to wrap round her neck or put on her knees.

I remember when she was wrapping it up she said, "John, I would love this for myself."

Well, she got her wish. We got it back with a note to the effect she hadn't got to that age yet.

No comment.

Anne always left me to think what to give my dad. Not that he would have minded if I had only wished him a Happy Christmas.

One year I sent him a shaving brush. He thanked me and said he would put it with the rest. I soon discovered there were five brand new shaving brushes in the bathroom. In fact, I'm using one of his today!

by John Taylor

"Why?"

"Because I've done everything I set out to do and it's time for a change. There are lots of people who can play well, but —" He smiled ruefully. "I've changed direction, from musician to composer. I'm about to start work on a film score."

He looked at her, as if he was waiting for her to say something. Gail, however, wasn't sure what he was saying, never mind what he expected her to say.

"Gail —" He put his coffee cup down and ran a hand through his hair.

"Perhaps you were right when you said I couldn't turn my back on

145

Paris. Perhaps I would have spent the rest of my life wondering what I could have achieved. But in everything else, I think you were wrong. We were in such a mess when I left, and you wouldn't answer my letters.

"For me, the last four years have been pointless. It might sound very glamorous, all the travelling. But without someone to share it with, a life like that is meaningless."

He gazed at her face and saw the confusion there.

"Am I making any sense, or has the jet-lag really hit me? Gail, I'm trying, very badly I know, to tell you how I feel. What about you? Have you been happy? Is there someone else in your life?"

"No, I haven't been particularly happy," she admitted softly, "and no, there's no-one else in my life. There was someone — up until last night — but no-one special."

H E crossed the room in two strides.
"Do you still feel the same? Do you still love me?"
"Yes."

He took her in his arms and covered her face with kisses.

"So you'll marry me?"

"Richard?" She didn't know whether to laugh or cry and she ended up doing a bit of both. "You can't see someone after four years and ask them to marry you."

"Why not?" Laughing, with all outward signs of weariness gone, he lifted her off her feet and swung her round.

"Because you have to think these things through. We might have changed. And marriage — how will you feel being married to someone who can't even play a recorder?"

"I've thought of marriage for six years, Gail. And of course we haven't changed."

"Yes, but —"

"I grew up in a house where it was impossible to hear yourself think. My idea of heaven is spending the rest of my days with someone who's content to listen, where I don't have to compete with a cornet in the next room, or three violins across the hall. Besides," he teased, "you're good for my ego. You tell me I'm brilliant because you're not a musician! You even think I can play the saxophone."

"You can. I've heard you."

"No, you've heard me make an unholy racket." He kissed her again. "Will you marry me, Gail?"

She longed to say yes, but it was absurd.

"I'll think about it."

"How long will that take?" He looked at his watch and she laughed.

"I'll tell you on your birthday," she promised and he seemed satisfied.

"So we'll be married — when? A month after my birthday?"

"I haven't said yes yet!"

"But you will."

And of course, she did. □

146

MOTHER'S LITTLE SECRET

YOU should see it, Becky! There's a tiny wreath on the front door and a Christmas tree in the drawing-room all decorated with —"

"I don't like doll's houses." The strawberry-blonde head was buried deep in a book of science experiments. "And please, Mum, I told you — Rebecca."

"Sorry, darling. It's a habit."

One that Megan had been loth to break. The nickname seemed about the only remnant of the babyhood bond she'd once felt with her daughter.

"She's a bright girl," her teacher had said on parents' evening. "Good with her hands, and very down to earth."

"Unlike her mother!" Megan had laughed nervously.

by Deborah Siepmann

147

"But it's no joke," she'd told Steve later that weekend. "We're just — so different."

"People are," Steve answered, with more than a touch of exasperation in his voice. "She's doing well at school and she's not in any trouble. Doesn't that make you happy?"

"Of course it does. It's just that —"

"What?"

"Oh, I don't know, Steve."

But she did know. In her heart, Megan had wanted a shy, dreamy child whom she could nurture and bring out slowly, like a fragile hothouse flower. Someone whose weaknesses might make her feel bolder and stronger.

Holding the newborn Rebecca, she'd imagined them together, sharing secrets and dreams, delighting in dainty shoes, party dresses and beautiful dolls . . .

But Rebecca's feet always ended up in the clumsiest of shoes. She had resisted pretty dresses from the age of two. And last term, a three-way negotiation on the playground had resulted in her neglected doll collection being swapped for a set of Lego.

Confident and determined, nine-year-old Rebecca often left Megan feeling almost intimidated. It had been against her better judgment that she'd mentioned the doll's house at all, but she simply hadn't been able to resist sharing her new discovery.

THE shop had opened on a dreary day in late November, when Megan's mood had matched the weather. She'd had more than a fair share of irritable customers to deal with at the dry cleaners', as if it were her own fault that the machinery had broken down.

As she'd stepped off the bus and started down the road for home, her eye had caught the newly-painted shop front. The place had been empty for ages, but now, with its cheerful face-lift, and shelves lined with beautifully furnished doll's houses, it seemed to light up the whole road.

Megan had walked slowly across the wide pavement, drawn to the magical world through the window. She'd stood there, almost in a trance . . .

Since that day, it had become her private ritual, stopping to take note of any new developments in the sumptuous mansion occupied by a small porcelain family she'd christened the Posselthwaites. It was something to look forward to, escaping for a few minutes each day.

Daydreams had always been her solace and retreat. Shrinking to the size of the Posselthwaites and stepping into their world couldn't have been a more enticing or timely fantasy. It seemed that the dry-cleaning machinery wasn't the only breakdown in Megan's life.

As Steve had said when the offer had come up, it wasn't a new woman taking him away during the week, it was a new job. He was, of course, thrilled with the opportunity to set up a northern branch of the computer shop where he'd worked for the last ten years. Perhaps, she'd thought, the fresh start might give their marriage a second wind.

It had been a long time since Steve had looked at her with the protective adoration he once had in the early days of their marriage. Megan had seen him then as her white knight, ready to save her from a world she'd found too harsh and fraught with unpredictability.

But it seemed there was a limit to the number of dragons that he could slay. And her dreaminess, which had once so enchanted him, had grown to be a source of exasperation.

So, although Megan had dared to tell Rebecca about the new shop, alarm bells kept her from mentioning it to Steve. He would almost certainly find her latest fantasy world thoroughly irritating.

His weekend homecomings hadn't been the second honeymoons Megan had hoped for. She was beginning to wonder if the distance between them at the weekend was greater than the miles which separated them during the week.

And so her daily visits to the Posselthwaites had become all the more treasured — secret and illicit . . .

ON the afternoon of Christmas Eve, Megan found herself thinking of her after-work assignation with the excitement of a longed-for Christmas treat.

She'd tried to get into the holiday spirit, shopping for presents and decorating the house, but it had all felt forced and contrived. Despite her clever hands, Rebecca had shown little interest this year in making decorations, or helping with the Christmas baking.

In fact, during the two weeks before school had broken up for the holidays, she'd been spending most of her free time at her friend Sophie's house. When Megan had suggested that Sophie come to their house sometimes, Rebecca had been evasive and looked uncomfortable.

Sophie's mother, Gillian, had offered, then, to look after Rebecca for the few days of holiday time between the end of term and Megan's last day of work. It would save hiring a child minder and, of course, she felt grateful to know Rebecca was so welcome.

The snag was that Megan had never felt at ease with the stylish Gillian, who worked from home as an interior decorator. Now, it seemed, Rebecca preferred Sophie's household to her own!

Well, she thought, hanging up the unclaimed dry-cleaning and putting on her coat, it's finally here — Christmas Eve.

She switched off the lights, turned the key in the lock and started off towards the bus stop.

The bus careered along the road, crowded with last-minute shoppers. She managed to find a seat and, as she settled herself someone turned up the volume on a transistor radio.

"Here's an oldie — Bing Crosby with a message for all of you waiting at home." The crooning voice sang out the poignant melody:

I'll be home for Christmas,
You can count on me . . .

THEY would be having Christmas on their own this year. Megan's parents had died some years ago, and Steve's were spending the holiday abroad. Gillian would bring Rebecca home, Steve would be back by six and then it would be the three of them, undiluted, for the holiday.

Hitching her handbag on to her shoulder, she made her way to the door of the bus.

Gillian would have to come in for a cup of tea, she thought regretfully, then immediately felt ashamed of such an unseasonal thought. But it was the last straw, making conversation with this perfect mother, creator of a domestic paradise.

Running across the road to her beloved window, she let the floodgates of comfort open wide as she lost herself once again. Slowly, the warm glow of the Posselthwaites' Christmas wrapped itself round her.

She gazed in at the little family, frozen in their contentment. Tiny stockings "hung by the chimney with care" while Mr Posselthwaite, clad in velvet dressing-gown, read the microscopic print of his newspaper.

Upstairs in the nursery, Mrs Posselthwaite stood poised over her baby's lace-swathed crib, just as Megan herself had once doted over little Rebecca.

Finally she turned up the collar of her coat against the sharp wind, took a last look and started for home. As she let herself into the house, the phone was ringing.

"Mum — it's me."

"Darling! Can't wait to see you. Is Sophie's mother about to bring you home?"

There was a pause.

"I'm not quite ready to come home yet . . ."

Megan took a breath. There it was again, the reluctance to be home — even on Christmas Eve.

"We're in the middle of a game," Rebecca finished.

"A game?" Megan said weakly.

"Please, Mum! I'll be back soon."

"But, Rebecca —"

"Bye!" she chirped, and hung up.

Slowly, Megan replaced the receiver. She felt a lump swell in her throat, and then the tears began to flow as disappointment and loneliness spread through her.

At last the doorbell rang. Megan blew her nose, and in a panic began to paw through her handbag for her make-up.

As she dabbed her face, the bell went again. She hurried to the door.

Rebecca was on the doorstep alone, no car in sight.

"Darling —"

Rebecca looked strangely shy; almost frightened.

"Hi, Mum." She took a breath and bit her lip, then stepped into the house.

"Sophie's mum said she was sorry not to see you. She was in a rush, so

150

Colin Gibson's Almanac

November

NOVEMBER is not always a dark and dreary month, but I remember a year when the rain hardly stopped. If we didn't have it in one form, we had it in another.

Drizzle and downpour, sending drifts and interweaving veils of wetness, heavy mists and thundery deluges.

At night we had rain hitting the windowpanes like gravel. By day, it dribbled on, hour after hour.

No wonder our rivers and streams, slow to rise after the summer drought, now brimmed their banks and began to overflow them.

Many rivers lost themselves in extensive lakes, and covered farm tracks, fields and pastures. The banks of many a stream were marked only by lines of trees.

At Killin, at the head of Loch Tay, I went to see the Falls of Dochart. These falls, or rapids, can be seen from the road — in fact, only the road separates the Falls from Killin's line of cottages. Even from the village, the roar of the rushing water is quite loud.

Normally, at this part of its course, the river is divided by rocky inlets, and is strikingly picturesque as it goes foaming this way and that.

But, on this occasion, the inlets were completely overwhelmed by the flood of waters, and the course of the river was in wild turmoil. Its roar was deafening and it was a memorable scene!

The Falls Of Dochart.

she dropped me off."

"Oh, I see." Megan felt simultaneous relief and hurt.

She began to move quickly about the room, switching on the Christmas tree lights, plumping cushions, busying herself. Rebecca stood as if fixed to the floor, with the same nervous expression.

Then, suddenly, her cheeks grew pink and she flew out of the room towards the kitchen. Megan thought she heard the back door open and then close again.

"Rebecca — what are you —?"

"Mum! Could you come through now?"

"Rebecca, are you all right?"

There was no answer. Megan felt herself break into a sweat and hurried to the kitchen with visions of Rebecca sick, or even sprawled out

151

on the floor . . .

But Rebecca wasn't any of those things.

"Happy Christmas, Mum." She seemed unlike herself — shy even. "I couldn't wait till Christmas morning. I didn't know how I could hide it!"

Beside Rebecca stood a doll's house.

It was made of four large cardboard boxes, with windows cut out on the sides. Each box was lined with a different pattern of wallpaper, with curtains to match.

The outside was covered in red poster paint with black lines, to look like brick. There was a long strip of cardboard folded in accordion pleats to form a staircase, and each room was filled with furniture and accessories, all made of matchboxes, cotton reels, bits of balsa wood and scraps of fabric.

"I made it — for you." Rebecca's eyes were very bright.

Megan opened her mouth to speak, but couldn't find her voice.

Rebecca seemed unaware of her mother's silence.

"I remembered you liked that shop — the one you told me about with the posh doll's houses. And one day I was at Sophie's and her mum had a lot of wine delivered for a party she was having. These big boxes gave me the idea.

"Sophie's mum gave me some bits of wallpaper and stuff from her work, and I started working every day. That's why I kept going over to Sophie's.

"Then, this afternoon, the staircase fell apart, so I had to stay longer, but I fixed it. Sophie's mum dropped me off so I could put it outside the back door to surprise you."

She paused, adjusting one of the curtains.

"I don't really like doll's houses, but this was like architecture. I'd never want one for myself," she went on, rearranging the furniture. "I mean, not to play with or anything. But I thought you might like it."

Old Tom Noggins

OLD TOM NOGGINS looks over the fence,
  On the corner of Meadowside Way,
A picture of donkey innocence,
  With his coat so shaggy and grey.
And everyone loves to see him there,
  So small and sweet, with his gentle air.

One day, as we stroked the velvet ears,
  Along the farmer came,
And when the children enquired of him:
  "What is your donkey's name?"
He cocked his eye, and he scratched his head,
  "Why, Old Tom Noggins will do!" he said.

If only Old Tom could talk, I'm sure
  He would tell us a tale or two,
Of his mischievous, madcap, merry youth,
  And the naughty things he'd do,
For, it is whispered, in his day,
  Our Tom was a regular tearaway!

152

Mother's Little Secret

Still unable to find words, Megan took her daughter gently by the shoulders and gathered her into her arms. She had to blink back the fresh tears which had begun to blur the picture she would remember forever.

"It's absolutely beautiful . . . completely amazing," she said at last. "Thank you, Rebecca. It's the most wonderful present I've ever been given — except, of course, for you."

"Oh, Mum, I wasn't a present — I'm a person!"

Megan laughed.

"You certainly are." She knelt in front of the doll's house.

"It's incredibly clever. And all that time at Sophie's, you were working so hard." She picked up a tiny rocking chair, marvelling at the detail. "And how nice of Gillian to give you the wallpaper and things!"

"She asked if I needed any help, but I wanted to do it all myself."

"Oh, Mum, I forgot — she said she wants to get together with you sometime during the holidays — have coffee or something. She said something weird about wanting 'to know your secret'. What did she mean?"

Megan smiled.

"Well, I'm not sure what secret she had in mind, but I'll tell you one now. I think we're going to have a wonderful Christmas, the best ever. And won't it be fun when Daddy gets home?"

She gazed into the doll's house. A perfect little world, part of a big one that was far from perfect. But with the imperfections would come the surprises; little everyday miracles. She was sure of that now.

In the safe and ordered world of make-believe, Steve would have been her dragon slayer and Rebecca her ivory tower companion, but they might all have missed the best kind of magic. Daydreams were fine for the odd visit, but they weren't for living in.

Perhaps, she thought, it was time to give the real world a chance . . . □

But Old Tom Noggins is wiser now,
  Content to dream in the sun,
He never would steal your cap, or scarf,
  Then kick up his heels, and run!
Or open the gate, and go wandering down
To cause traffic jams in our little town!

Though such a rapscallion in his day,
Now, he just steals your heart away. . .
  — Kathleen O'Farrell.

A Wedding Has B

DORA WARD stepped out into the garden. It was a balmy summer evening and the scent of stocks and old-fashioned roses followed her down the path to the gnarled old pear tree at the bottom of the garden.

Under it was a rustic seat where Dora liked to sit, to take in the familiar sight of the village with its backdrop of rolling fells. Beyond the garden hedge a path, which on evenings such as this, was a favourite haunt for courting couples.

The sun was setting in a blaze of gold and crimson.

"Red sky at night, shepherd's delight," she quoted to Barney, the cat, who'd appeared out of nowhere to weave around her legs. "Fine again tomorrow."

by Pamela Kavanagh

Barney jumped on to her lap and curled up. The garden breathed quietly around them, birds settling for the night and flowers silently closing their petals.

Suddenly, the sound of voices raised in argument drifted over the hedge.

"But, James, I've set my heart on a white wedding! I know it'll be expensive, but it's once in a lifetime — a special day."

"So we can make it special without the frills, can't we, Lucy?" the unseen James replied reasonably.

"Take the dress. How much is that going to be? Five hundred? A thousand? It's crazy to spend all that on something you'll only wear a matter of hours."

"It isn't crazy." Lucy's voice was mutinous. "I'll treasure my dress — if I ever get one, that is!"

"That money could buy roof timbers and bricks. What's more important — a home to live in, or a frock that'll be stored away in a cupboard?"

Put like that, the young man did have a point, Dora thought. On the other hand, so did Lucy . . .

Dora shifted uneasily in her seat, realising she was eavesdropping. But Barney was sleeping contentedly, a warm furry black ball on her lap, so she continued to sit, hoping the couple would move on.

"Look," James tried again, "if a wedding dress means so much, why not make one yourself? The bridesmaids' as well.

"There'll be other ways we can economise, too — the flowers, the reception. We can still make it your special day."

"Our special day!" Lucy corrected.

Dora heard the suspicion of a tremor in the girl's voice and her heart tugged in sympathy.

Arranged

J. Hancock.

"Think about it, eh?" James said encouragingly. "Look, I've got to go, love. I have to see about cementing the foundations for the house. Then, a few more evenings like this and we'll have the walls up. Great, isn't it?"

"Mmm," came Lucy's response. "I might stop here a while. Dad's not expecting me back. 'Bye then."

James left, whistling cheerfully as he strode off down the lane.

Dora felt herself relax.

Then she heard the sob, stifled at first, but becoming more distressed.

Cautiously putting the cat aside, she got up and went to the hedge.

"Er . . . young woman . . . Lucy!" she called. "Are you all right?"

"Oh . . . I . . ." Lucy jumped. "It's you, Mrs Ward! Yes, I'm fine, thanks. Absolutely fine!" As she said it, she burst into a fresh storm of tears.

"Dear dear," Dora said. "You just come along inside. I'll have the kettle on in two shakes."

TEN minutes later, the two women sat at Dora's kitchen table. "There. Help yourself to milk and sugar. Biscuit?" "No, thanks." Lucy raised her pretty tear-stained face for a moment.

She'll make a lovely bride, Dora thought.

"Erm, I couldn't help but overhear — I often sit outside of an evening. You and your young fellow having a few problems it seems?"

"I know James is right." Lucy nodded miserably.

"We've bought this building plot on the other side of the village. James is a builder, so it seemed daft to go buying a house when he could make us something better for less cost."

"Very sensible." Dora sipped her tea.

"Yes." Lucy heaved a sigh. "We're very fortunate."

"It's not that I'm ungrateful, but I would so love a proper wedding. Mum would have seen things my way — but she's not here any more and Dad's already helped us to buy the plot. A wedding's so expensive, the flowers, the dress and everything, but . . ."

"Let's think this out." Dora topped up the cups. "Of course, you could always do as your James suggests and make the dress. Lots of girls do."

"Not my friends," Lucy protested. "I suppose you did?"

A glimmer of a smile crossed Dora's thin face.

"No, it was wartime then. I wore my best frock and my Alf was in uniform. But, like you, I had my dreams. Daresay I'd have made one if it was possible."

"Well, I couldn't," Lucy muttered. "I'm useless at sewing. I wouldn't know where to start."

"With a pattern," Dora heard herself say. "And a few yards of material and my old sewing machine."

"Oh!" Hope shone in Lucy's eyes. "Could you help me with it?

"James is going to be occupied with the bungalow from now on, so I've got most evenings free. The wedding isn't until late September. Oh, please say you will?"

It was a plea for help that Dora couldn't ignore.

Next evening, Lucy arrived laden with a large parcel of shimmery watered silk, tiny pearl buttons and a pattern.

"Let's see what you've got," Dora said. "It's not too fancy, is it?"

Lucy had sensibly chosen a straightforward design.

Night after night, with a little help from Dora, she laboured over the delicate fabric. She snipped and pinned, tacked and fitted, until at last it was time to sew the seams of the dress.

"I never thought sewing could be this much fun," Lucy admitted one evening. They were placing the sleeves, not an easy task.

"I'm tempted to make my bridesmaids' dresses as well — if that's all right?"

"It's up to you, love," Dora said. "You're the seamstress."

"Oh no, not really. I just follow your advice. I could never do it on my own."

"Better get the material then, hadn't you? Two, wasn't it? Your best friend, Anne, and Elizabeth, James' little sister. Have you decided on a colour yet?"

"Something soft. Pink perhaps? They're both blonde so it should suit, but I'll check with them first."

"Now that the dresses have been taken care of, what about the flowers? If you like, you can help yourself out of the garden," Dora said generously.

"But your garden's always such a picture. I wouldn't want to spoil it." Lucy sighed.

"Bless you, love." Dora smiled. "There are enough flowers to fill a cathedral and still have some over! Just you leave it to me. I'll take care of the flowers."

By mid-August, the wedding gown was finished. When Lucy tried it on, complete with veil, Dora gave a gasp of pleasure.

"My! That outfit is as good as any in the shops!"

All at once there didn't seem to be enough hours in the day. Dora began to wonder what she did with herself before Lucy needed her help. When she wasn't vacuuming snippets of white silk

Granny's Quilt

I WELL remember Granny's quilt,
Which lay upon her bed,
A galaxy of colours —
Blue and yellow, green and red.

Each square was sewn by Granny's hand,
As neat as neat can be,
And every tiny square of cloth
Held precious memory.

A bit of cotton skirt she wore,
In stripes of green and gold,
And velvet from her wedding gown,
So soft and fine and old.

Some flannel from a baby's gown,
And gingham which had been,
A very pretty party frock
When Gran was seventeen.

A piece of Grandpa's finest shirt,
Which Granny always said
Was that same shirt which Grandpa wore
The day that they got wed.

Among those precious fabrics found
In Granny's patchwork quilt,
Was just a touch of tartan from
Dear Grandpa's Army kilt.

But best of all, as Granny said,
Her patchwork quilt was fine
For holding close sweet memories,
Of days of Auld Lang Syne.
— Alice Drury.

from the carpet, she was outdoors, planning Lucy's bridal bouquet.

Hopefully, the pretty blush roses would be in their second bloom, then, with fern and a smattering of sweet peas, she could fashion arrangements fit for a queen. The posies were simple and would feature lovely lilies.

Compared with the bride's dress, the bridesmaids' outfits were quite simple — well, according to Lucy they were. Dora thought the girl had got the hang of sewing pretty well, considering it was all new to her.

"How's the bungalow coming on?" she inquired as they sat one evening over supper.

"Absolutely splendid, Dora. You must come over and see it."

"That's all right, love," Dora said. "I'm not one for going out, you know. I've not been outside the gate in years. After my Alf went, there was no-one to go out for, so I didn't bother."

"Oh, but that's awful." Lucy looked shocked. "What about shopping and everything?"

"Get it delivered. Maybe that's the reason. All too easy. I never had to make the effort and now . . ." She shrugged.

"Doesn't matter. Nobody misses an old woman, who can't bring herself to socialise!"

"I thought you were just a private sort of person," Lucy said. "You never seemed shy, not to me."

"Like I said, one has to make the effort. So what's next on the list?"
Dora began to tick off the items on her fingers.

"Bride's dress done, bridesmaids' all but done, bouquets in hand — ah, the refreshments?"

"No problem. We're having a sit-down meal, provided by the WI, at the village hall and a barn dance afterwards. One of James' mates plays in the band, and they're coming as a favour. I've made and iced my own cake — baking is something I *can* do!"

"Very handy," Dora said. "Is something wrong?"

All at once Lucy's face had crumpled in dismay.

"Oh, Dora, you've just got to be there. And at the church. All our friends are invited. It won't be the same without you."

Glenuig, Moidart

MOIDART, which lies on Scotland's west coast, gets its name from a combination of muid, meaning sea spray, and ard, a height — giving us "heights of the sea spray."

This romantic name suits the area perfectly, because as well as being a haven of peace and tranquility set in remote beauty, Moidart is irrevocably connected with dramatic events in Scottish history. It was here, in 1745, that The Young Pretender, Prince Charles Edward Stewart, landed to summon clansmen to form the Jacobite army.

GLENUIG, MOIDART : J CAMPBELL KERR

Dora felt herself go cold.

"I'll think about it," was all she said.

SIX days before the wedding, when everything was running smoothly, Lucy made one final attempt to persuade her friend. "Please, Dora. If you don't come, you won't see us in all our finery. All your hard work . . . your wonderful sewing."

"Don't you bother about me, love." Dora shook her head. "I'll be at the gate to watch you go past in the car. I'll be too busy anyway, putting the finishing touches to the flowers, to get ready in time."

Sighing, Lucy changed the subject. "What's your favourite colour?"

"Pale blue," Dora said promptly. "Why?"

"Never you mind." Lucy smiled.

For the next few days, Dora saw nothing of her young friend. Busy with last-minute plans, she told herself.

She was occupied herself, sketching and re-sketching a design for the bouquet. At last, she had it perfected.

Dora's wedding gift to Lucy and James was a bone china tea-set that had been a wedding present to her and Alf. Lucy had often admired it and Dora knew she and James would treasure it.

On the morning of the wedding, Dora rose before the dawn mist had cleared, picking the best of the chosen flowers for the bouquets, posies and buttonholes. She'd already completed the arrangements for the church which Lucy had put in place late last night. By now the garden was looking decidedly bare.

In the kitchen, Dora, surrounded by flowers, was about to start work when she heard a noise outside. Going to investigate, she found, hanging on the door-knob and covered in polythene, a smart, two-piece in a delicate shade of pale blue. Pinned to it was a note.

Dearest Dora,

I made this specially. PLEASE come. James has arranged for you to sit in a quiet corner of the church where you can see what's going on, but you won't be too noticeable.

Love, Lucy.

Dora's eyes misted at Lucy's thoughtfulness. Then she panicked. What was she to do?

Hastily, she put the question to the back of her mind. She'd get on with the bouquets and posies and see how the time went, then she'd decide.

HEADS turned as the organ struck up and the bride entered the church with her father. Lucy looked a picture in the dress of flowing silk, the veil a gauzy froth about her happy face and the bouquet a splash of vibrant colour.

Following, the bridesmaids looked lovely, too. Pretty, but not overshadowing the bride.

Seated in a quiet corner behind a screen of her own familiar flowers,

A Wedding Has Been Arranged . . .

Dora smiled until her face ached.

What a girl Lucy was! Almost the daughter she had never had. And James, getting up at the crack of dawn to sort out her 'arbour'!

Clearing his throat, the vicar intoned the opening words.

"Dearly beloved, we are gathered here today . . ."

Dora glanced down at her hands, resting on her pale blue skirt. Such clumsy hands. Hands that had rarely held a needle, let alone worked a sewing machine!

Confidence, that was all Lucy needed to sew that dress. And, Dora thought, it's all that I needed, too. A little bit of confidence.

What a day, Dora concluded, as she joined the congregation in standing for the first hymn. A special day all round . . . □

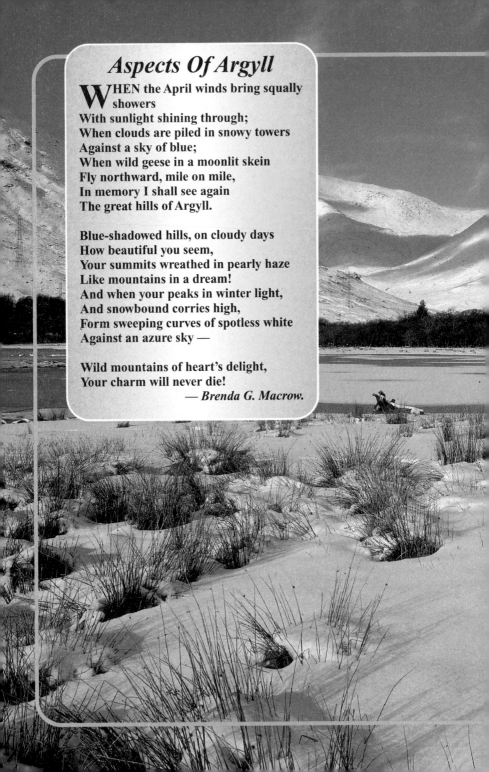

Aspects Of Argyll

WHEN the April winds bring squally
    showers
With sunlight shining through;
When clouds are piled in snowy towers
Against a sky of blue;
When wild geese in a moonlit skein
Fly northward, mile on mile,
In memory I shall see again
The great hills of Argyll.

Blue-shadowed hills, on cloudy days
How beautiful you seem,
Your summits wreathed in pearly haze
Like mountains in a dream!
And when your peaks in winter light,
And snowbound corries high,
Form sweeping curves of spotless white
Against an azure sky —

Wild mountains of heart's delight,
Your charm will never die!
            — *Brenda G. Macrow.*

Kilchurn Castle, Loch Awe.

Dennis Hardley.

by Pamela Lyons

In The Summer Of '39

Barcilon.

I MADE two mistakes the summer I was fifteen. One, I fell in love with Reginald Baker. Two, I never told him.

Strictly speaking, you couldn't say falling in love was a mistake because, when you're fifteen, these things just happen.

Let's say it was unfortunate. You see Reginald, "Red" to his friends, was only interested in one girl — Meg, my elder sister. That was the reason I could never let him know how I felt about him. It was all too complicated.

Still, that summer of 1939 turned out to be memorable for more serious reasons than my thwarted love. But I was young, and far too preoccupied with my own small world to worry about what was going on in the big wide world, far away in Europe.

My entire life was taken over that summer by my burgeoning emotions. Or, more simply, by Red Baker.

Everyone called him Red

laughed a great deal.

Of course, I wasn't the only girl in our small Suffolk village to find him attractive. But until I found out about his feelings for my sister, I didn't care. In my girlish dreams, we were already promised to each other.

I knew, in my heart of hearts, it was only a matter of time before Red would acknowledge our destiny, declare his undying love for me, and we'd live happily ever after.

At fifteen, you don't think Fate plays cruel games. You walk around with stars in your eyes, the sky is always blue — the future bright and sunny. It was Meg who brought me back down to earth.

"Guess what?" My sister had bounced into the house happy as a summer's day. "Red Baker's asked me out!"

I was surprised no-one heard my world collapse.

"But . . . but, you can't!" I'd stammered. Turning in desperation to my mother, who was sewing the hem of my gymslip, I'd blurted out, "Tell her, Mum!"

"Tell Meg what, Sally, dear?" My mother had understandably looked confused.

because of his rust-coloured hair. Red also had broad shoulders, and pale blue eyes which twinkled when he laughed. I seem to remember, in those halcyon days before the war, Red smiled and

"Why, that — oh never mind!" My cheeks had grown hot, while tears of frustration stung my eyes.

Meg's hazel eyes had widened. She was petite and pretty, like our mother. And she didn't have any pimples.

Realising something far more serious was going on than at first met the eye, my mother had left her sewing.

"Is there a reason why Meg shouldn't go out with Red?" she'd inquired sensibly. "Something I should know about?"

"Well, Sally?" Meg's creamy complexion had pinkened.

They both waited, watching me, while I'd died inside.

"Red Baker is always going out with girls," I'd spluttered at last. "Lots of girls." The implication was obvious.

Anyway, what I'd said was true. But there was a reason. Apart from his film star good looks, Red had another very important asset: a bicycle. A brand new, shiny black bicycle with chrome handlebars, which his parents had bought him for his nineteenth birthday.

It was the envy of all his friends. The favoured few were allowed to ride it round the village green. Some of the girls actually got to sit on the crossbar with Red pedalling them round the Mill Pond, or down secluded Church Lane.

Of course, I hadn't been one of those girls. I was fifteen, wore ankle socks, had pigtails, and certainly wasn't a candidate for clandestine bicycle rides with the local heart-throb.

Besides, my secret longings were one thing, but I would have died if Red had so much as looked at me.

All my turbulent emotions were thrashing around, willing Red to sweep me away on a white charger — or his bicycle! — while the shy, insecure child deep within was still pretending all boys were horrid.

My mother, in her usual astute manner, had summed up the situation. She'd put aside her sewing, suggesting we all had tea and Meg had quickly followed her.

Typically, I'd run up to my room, thrown myself over the patchwork quilt, and burst into tears.

THE pain of my unrequited love consumed me that long summer. At fifteen, a broken heart doesn't allow much room for anything else. I was vaguely aware of my father's conversations about "a German-Soviet pact of non-aggression". But it didn't mean anything to me because I was feeling particularly aggressive each time I heard my mother talk excitedly about Meg "blossoming" into a lovely young woman.

"Do you think your Meg and my brother are going to get engaged?" my best friend Pauline Baker whispered, one Sunday morning, in church.

"Don't be so stupid!" I'd hissed.

"No need to be rude!" Pauline had looked quite hurt. "I'm only repeating what other people are saying."

"Well, other people should keep their noses out of other people's

Colin Gibson's Almanac

December

IT'S years ago now, but how pleasant it was, after a turn on the hill, to sit by the shepherd's fireside — a yellow-eyed collie at my feet — and watch the red landscape of the burning logs.

Aye, it's something we never experience nowadays. The old-fashioned fireplace with its swey and three-legged pot has become a thing of the past.

Sitting in the firelight these days, my thoughts turn to some of the hill shepherds I've known. There was Jim Colville — I met him in Glenesk many years ago — a fine man and a good shepherd. On old maps, his house was called "Between Ye Burns" — two hill burns met nearby.

I got Jim to sit for his portrait, and I sketched him (though he didn't know it) at the sheep buchts and on the hill.

Out with him, tending the ewes, often in the very worst of weather, I found I could share something of that sense of guardianship that a shepherd feels for his flock.

It's not surprising that shepherds figure so largely in the Christmas story, or that the Holy Child named Jesus came to be called The Lamb of God and The Good Shepherd.

I remember, when I left the cottage on that December afternoon, the red-gold sun had set behind the birchwood and hill to the west.

They were singing carols at the village church — clear young voices — and a glittering star was rising in the east.

An old-fashioned fireplace.

affairs!" I'd raised my hymn book to cover my face and hide the shameful tears filling my eyes.

"It would be so romantic!" Pauline sighed.

I hadn't replied. I was too busy swallowing the lump in my throat.

AS the summer progressed, the news on the wireless began to concentrate more and more on the probability of another war. "It won't be like the last one," my father had remarked, over cold Sunday lunch. "If there is a war, they won't be saying this time that it'll all be over by Christmas."

My mother had turned pale. "Let's pray they all see sense, John."

The People's Friend Annual

Determined to change the subject, she'd glanced pointedly at my plate of untouched food.

"Sally, please eat your lunch. You're far too skinny. Are you sure you're not sickening for something?"

"I'm fine. I'm just not hungry." I arranged a lettuce leaf over the slice of cold ham.

Who would want to eat with everyone talking about war? Besides, how could I eat when my heart was broken?

Meg, on the other hand, was always ravenous. Talk of Germany intending to invade Poland didn't dull her appetite. All she seemed interested in was dressing up, trying out the latest hairstyle copied from movie magazines, and plastering her mouth with crimson lipstick.

When she wasn't in front of a mirror, she was out with Red and his friends. She went picnicking, played tennis, swam in Mill Pond or went to the cinema, while I was left at home.

"CHEER up, darling," my mother said, catching me one afternoon, curled up on my bedroom window seat, staring out at the world from my self-imposed prison.

"It won't be long before you'll be dressing up and going out, too." She'd stroked her fingers through my hair.

"But it's not fair!" I'd blurted out, burying my face in her soft cotton skirt.

She'd smelt of soap and rose water, and, at that moment, I think I loved her more than anyone on earth — except the boy with the laughing blue eyes and copper hair.

"Believe me, sweetheart, in a year from now everything will be very different." My mother had dried my tears.

Looking back, I don't think she ever realised how prophetic her words had been.

* * * *

Sunday, September 3. While we were all in church, the Prime Minister, Neville Chamberlain, had informed the nation a state of war had existed between Britain and Germany for over an hour. The sombre news soon swept through the congregation.

It was the beginning of the end of the old world as we all knew it. I think it was also the last day of my childhood.

After the service, we had walked home in silence. My parents ahead, arm-in-arm. As we turned down Church Lane, Meg slipped her fingers through mine and gave my hand a gentle squeeze.

Surprised, I had been about to snatch it away when I saw she was crying softly.

"Meg. What is it?" I felt my own tears of sympathy welling up.

It was only later, after the years of destruction, of air raids and bombings — of lost lives and shattered dreams — that I came to understand just what I was crying for on that memorable September morning.

A FEW weeks later, walking back from the general store across the village green, the sudden squelch of rubber tyres on the damp turf made me turn round.

"Hello, Sally." Red's muscular legs straddled his bicycle. His blue cotton shirt contrasted against his summer-bronzed skin and highlighted his clear eyes.

Before I could reply, he'd swung his leg over the crossbar.

"Mind if I walk with you? I have to see Meg."

Tongue-tied, as usual, I'd simply nodded. Close to, he was even more devastatingly handsome. He smelt of summer grass and ripe hay, glowing with health and an innate strength.

"I suppose you'll be back at school soon?" His voice was husky, soft as honey.

I was acutely aware of my baggy white shorts, my skinny bare legs; of my unfashionable sleeveless blouse and breeze-blown hair. Again, miserably, I nodded.

"I expect Meg has told you I'm joining up?"

I'd stopped abruptly, then turned to face him.

"I see she hasn't." His expression became more serious. "I'm joining the Royal Air Force Volunteer Reserve." His foot kicked at a tuft of grass.

"I report to a new RAF station in Norfolk tomorrow . . ."

His words became more measured, as if he began to realise the enormity of what he was about to do.

We stood, silently facing each other. I don't recall anything about that moment other than we were out of time in a safe, secret place, just the two of us. Somewhere far away, the real world was going mad.

As Red reached out to wipe the tears off my cheek, the spell was broken.

"Sally?" A million unformed questions lay behind Red speaking my name.

A desperate sadness swept over me, forcing me to turn, to race across the grass. I was just sixteen, far too young for the flood of emotions which threatened to overwhelm me. Too shy to confess I loved him.

* * * *

A month after Red had left the village, Meg announced she was volunteering for the Women's Land Army.

"But you don't know anything about farming," I'd replied.

"Well, it's time I learned." Noticing our mother's look of disapproval, she'd added, "Many of the local farms will need workers, so I won't need to move away."

"Besides," for a moment, she'd stared wistfully through the window at the autumn-tinted afternoon, "I need to feel useful." She had forced a

Loch Morlich and The Cairngorms.

bright smile. "After all, as everyone says, there is a war on, you know."

"If you want to contribute towards the war effort," Mother said, "I'll need plenty of help around here."

Meg had shaken her head. "I'm sorry, Mum. But I'm not the type to knit socks for sailors. I can't sit round worrying about Red and all the others. I have to do something."

I'd wondered what she'd really felt. At least she had Red's letters, which she shared — in part. But she still went out with her friends and spent hours in front of the dressing-table mirror pinning up her hair or arranging it to fall over her face, like Veronica Lake. So I couldn't see how she missed Red that much. But I did.

Blue Remembered Hills

MOUNTAINS of amethyst,
Topaz and cairngorm,
Great hanging corries and steep granite screes,
Cloud-girdled summits,
Fast-flowing rivers,
Deeply carved glens amid billowing trees!

Mountains of legend,
Moody Macdui,
Haunt of the Grey Man who walks in the mist!
Grizzled Braeriach
Guarding the Lairig,
Dark pools of the Dee by the summer sun kissed!

Red deer are shadows
High on the hillside,
Mountain hares hide where the bright heather
    blows.
Fierce golden eagles
Circle the summits,
Ptarmigan blend with the lingering snows.

Blue hills of beauty,
Loved by the climber,
Skier's delight when the winter sun gleams —
Far from your glories,
Still we remember
  Vistas of splendour that stay in our dreams!
                              — *Brenda G. Macrow.*

Dennis Hardley.

I was in the house, alone, when I heard someone calling from the front door.

I ran through to the hall, hardly daring to believe it was Red. But it was.

He leaned nonchalantly against the porch in his airforce blue uniform. The top button of his tunic was undone and a white scarf was knotted round his neck.

He seemed different, somehow. Older. Yet, the moment he smiled, the year since I'd last seen him rolled away.

I was sixteen again — and we were on the common — lost in our secret place.

"Flying Officer Baker reporting." He gave a mock salute. "I've got a forty-eight hour stand-down, so — may I come in?"

I stepped forward to greet him as he walked into the hall. We met in the middle and stood close, facing each other. My thrill at seeing him again suddenly shadowed by the knowledge that the girl he really wanted to see — Meg — wouldn't be happy to see him.

"You've grown up, Sally. No more pigtails, eh?" Red walked round me, beaming. "You're becoming quite a stunner!"

As usual, I was tongue-tied, flustered. Mentally, I'd rehearsed this moment a hundred times. But all I could do was grin sheepishly while my heart was willing Red to sweep me into his arms.

Red did open his arms — but they weren't for me.

"Meg!"

He strode past me as my sister, dressed in old dungarees, blonde curls poking out beneath a scarf tied turban fashion round her head, walked into the room. Meg's surprise quickly turned to embarrassment.

"Red? What are you doing here? Didn't you get my letter?"

Her lack of enthusiasm chilled the room. Turning to me, she shrugged.

"Sally, I need to speak to Red. Do you mind leaving us alone?"

I did mind. I minded desperately. Ever since she'd started going out with Tom Morgan, the widower who owned Brook Farm, I'd minded. But what could I do? Meg was my sister and I loved her.

Yet I loved Red, too, and I'd hated having to stand by and say nothing. But I was good at that, wasn't I? I'd spent my life keeping silent, instead of speaking up.

I glared at my sister, then glanced across at Red.

I saw the apprehension register on his face, concern clouding his blue eyes. I couldn't bear to stay in the room a moment longer, so I turned and fled.

I DIDN'T see Red again until June, 1945. A month before, the war in Europe had ended.

After that fateful day when Meg had told him they were finished, his squadron had been moved near the south coast. All through the long, weary years of the war I had kept writing to him.

My letters read more like a diary, keeping him up to date with local news.

I wrote about the day the first delivery of bananas had sent us all stampeding across the village green to queue in the pouring rain. About my NAAFI duties at the nearby airforce base. About the effects of rationing and how we were all getting used to tea with condensed milk, of coffee made out of chicory.

I joked about making lentils look like duck, of how my mother's rose garden had been turned into a vegetable patch . . .

Sometimes, I'd receive a short letter back, a scribbled postcard. Mostly, there was nothing. All I had was the burning hope that one day, Red would come home.

In The Summer Of '39

The day after the village street party to celebrate VE Day, I was pushing the pram along Church Lane when I heard a bicycle bell clanging loudly behind me. I stepped aside, silently chiding whoever it was who was in such a hurry.

Then I turned and saw him. He was racing towards me on his old-fashioned black bicycle, the wind whipping his burnished hair.

He stopped as he came abreast of me, straddling the bike.

"Hello, Sally."

"Hello, Red," I replied easily.

"Lovely little boy." He peered into the pram.

"It's a girl." I laughed.

"She looks like Meg."

"She is Meg's."

Red grinned. I presumed Pauline must have told him. I hadn't filled him in with all the news. Such as Meg marrying Tom Morgan and having a baby. I hadn't thought it necessary — or kind.

Red leaned his bicycle against the church wall then walked across to join me.

"It's all over, Sally." He gave a wry grin.

I nodded. "Thank heavens. And you're home, safe."

For a moment, we were gazing at each other like awkward strangers.

"I don't mean just the war, Sally." For once, he sounded uncertain . . . shy. "I mean —" he hesitated. "I need to tell you . . . what I thought I felt for Meg is over."

"Yes?"

"A long time ago. Then, when I started getting your letters, everything fell into place." He reached out to touch my face.

I covered his hand with my own, holding his warm fingers against my cheek.

"It's you I love, Sally." He looked uncertain of my reaction as he went on.

"I've loved you for a long time. But I didn't want to tell you — not until the war was over. Until — well, I came home."

"I know." I smiled. Hadn't I always known we'd be together one day? Wasn't it our destiny?

As I walked into the circle of Red's waiting embrace, the baby gurgled, contentedly.

For once, I paid her no attention. I had waited seven long years to feel Red's arms around me and I was in no hurry to ever leave them. □

Printed and Published in Great Britain by D. C. Thomson & Co., Ltd., Dundee, Glasgow and London. © D. C Thomson & Co., 1999. While every reasonable care will be taken, neither D. C. Thomson & Co., Ltd., nor its agents will accept liability for loss or damage to colour transparencies or any other material submitted to this publication.
ISBN 0-85116-669-5
EAN 9-780851-166698

GOLD HILL, SHAFTESBURY :J CAMPBELL KERR